In Praise of Mr. Pete

The term "legend" is often reserved for someone who was extremely famous, especially in a particular field of endeavor and often on a national stage.

But while the late State Rep. Pete Turnham would have been the first person to say he never considered himself a legend — at least not in the "traditional sense" — one thing is absolutely certain... "Mr. Pete," as he was fondly known, was first and foremost a gentleman.

Moreover, during a time in our nation where political leaders are often better known for what they can tear down rather than build up, Rep. Pete Turnham was a statesman whose life and service were measured by the Golden Rule, mutual respect for both his colleagues and constituents, and a love of his nation, state, family and God... and not necessarily in that order!

"Mr. Pete" answered his country's call during World War II before returning home to serve his community and district as one of — if not — the longest-serving State Representatives in Alabama history. He became affectionately known as "the Dean of the House" and he was respected for being as effective at mastering the legislative process — especially from his perch as a member of the powerful Ways and Means Committee — as he was for being a man of great humility... quiet, thoughtful, genuine and honest as the day is long. If "Mr. Pete" told you it was raining outside, you might as well go grab you umbrella. He was an institution who always served the institution he loved with the highest degree of integrity and decency.

While we are all dealing with so many challenges in our day-to-day life, it is refreshing to recall a kind and gentle man, the gentleman from Auburn, Rep. Pete

Turnham. His story is of a truly remarkable life ... a life that needs to be emulated as often as possible by both seasoned pros and rookies as well. For someone who lived to almost 100, "Mr. Pete" left his mark... and we are all the better for it.

—Kay Ivey
Governor, State of Alabama

Mr. Pete Turnham was truly an icon in Alabama political and legislative history. During the later years of his 40 year legislative career, and after his retirement, he was referred to affectionately as the "Dean of the House". It was my fortune in life to sit next to Mr. Pete for 16 years in the State Legislature. We became fast and lifetime friends. You get to know someone well being together that long. He was truly the consummate Christian gentleman. He truly cared for people. He loved his wife, Kay, his children, his church, and Auburn. Pete Turnham made a difference during his century on earth. He epitomized the Greatest Generation.

—Steve Flowers
Former Alabama State Representative &
Syndicated Political Columnist

Mr. Pete

The Pete Turnham Story

written by
Ann Romine Wilder

Publishing services by Selah Publishing Group, LLC, Tennessee.

ISBN: 978-1-58930-315-7
LCCN:2020907165

Appreciation to the Author

The family especially salutes and thanks the author of Mr. Pete and fellow family member, Ann Romine Wilder.

Ann faithfully, and with great determination, carried forth this daunting project with much research, by putting the many oral stories into written words, and by highlighting over 130 photo images into the book.

Ann and her husband, Cecil, made many trips from Georgia to Auburn, Alabama to interview and record Mr. Pete, family members and former colleagues over several years in order to pull the book together.

Ann's parents were especially close to Mr. Pete and Pete shared a mutual love and admiration for Ann and all of her family.

Ann's devotion to the project has not only allowed Pete Turnham's many life experiences to be shared with generations of family and friends, but they have also chronicled a century of Alabama history for all readers to learn from and enjoy in the years ahead.

Contents

Appreciation to the Author. 5
Author's Grateful Appreciation To... 9
The Early Years 13
Leaving Home...19
The War Years..23
Getting Established and Making a Home.......................................37
Entering the Alabama House of Representatives............................43
The Southern States Energy Board..57
Autumn Saturdays and Auburn Football..69
Continuing to Move Forward and Take On More Responsibility.......73
Alabama Contract Sales, Inc...79
Continuing to Serve..83
Herb, Pete, and Auburn..87
Election Time Again..91
Ted, Pete, and the Legislature...103
Continuing to Expand Duties and Responsibilities.........................107
Bobby, Pete, and Adult Education..111
Honored As He Works...117
Steve and Pete - Side by Side..123
Moving Ahead and More Awards..127
Scott's Saturdays with Pete...139
Always Pushing Forward...143
Turnham Green...151
Wrapping Up a 40 Year Career...153
Moving Forward...159
Kay, Pete, and Carolyn..163

The Golden Years...165
Memories and Thoughts from Pete's Children............................169
Pete...181
    Epilogue 183
    Bibliography...187

Author's Grateful Appreciation To...

Dear friends, Cheryl Gregory and Pam Hendley, and my sweet daughter, Betsy Wilder Stuart, true experts who edited and made corrections and helpful suggestions;

Special friends, Nancy and Johnnie Vinson, who gave my husband and me a place to stay each time we visited Pete, met us for lunch when we were there for only a day, and helped me with research in the town of Auburn and at the University;

Scott Couch, Bobby Dees, Steve Flowers, Ted Little, Ken Nemeth, Carolyn Payne, and Herb White who graciously gave of their time to talk with me about their relationship with and love for Pete, each of whom I felt became a good friend;

Pete's children - Diane, who spent countless hours going through books, drawers, sacks, and boxes in her parents' home to find newspaper articles, programs, pictures, albums, letters, army papers, and other memorabilia which helped tell her father's story; Tim, who told me how Pete loved his company and how the two of them built the company together; Joe, who made many connections for me with the people he knew were key in telling his dad's story; and to Ruthmary for her enthusiasm about her daddy's story being told. All of them made the day magical when they sat down to tell me of their memories of growing up the sons and daughters of Pete and Kay;

Mark Wilder, my brother-in-law, who, with his excellent TV broadcasting voice, spent many hours recording the book so Pete could hear his story;

Ryan Barbee, who spent hours formatting the book with his trained and artistic eye;

To my beloved husband, Cecil, who scanned pictures and articles, was my computer expert and constant help due to my limited expertise, recorded most of my talks with Pete and others, made many trips with me to and from Auburn and to the state archives in Montgomery, and played the recordings of the book for Pete. Without his help and encouragement the book would not have happened.

for Pete

The Early Years

MOTHER:
FANNIE MAE "FAN" SESSIONS

On a blustery winter day in Penton, a community 85 miles northeast of Montgomery, Alabama, Pete Benton Turnham was born, the fifth child of Joseph Henry and Fannie Mae Sessions Turnham. Pete arrived on January 1, the first day of 1921, and he would become a mighty voice in the state of Alabama. Soon after his birth, the family of seven moved just over eight miles north to the community of Abanda, to be closer to the extended Sessions family. Abanda was founded in the early part of the century (the post office was established in 1908 and closed in 1957) when the Atlanta, Birmingham, and Atlantic Railroads (ABandA) were extended to that point. Pete's father, Mr. Henry, as he was often called, eked out a living farming the small parcel of land he owned in the red hills of Chambers County, and a new boy meant another

FATHER:
JOSEPH HENRY TURNHAM

back and pair of hands to help work that land. Living in a two room house, later expanded to four, and with Bill, the sixth and last child, born almost eight years after Pete, the older children helped take care of the younger ones, and all worked together to keep food on the table and clothes on their backs. In those early years, Mr. Henry sometimes had to go away to work for money to help support his family, often working on a large steam shovel, and his absence was difficult for all.

There was a wood-burning stove in the corner of one of the rooms, and a table sat nearby. Because there was not enough room for all to sit, some stood while the blessing was being said, and continued to stand while they ate, so that they could enjoy being together at mealtime. With no plumbing, there was an outhouse. Baths were taken, when weather permitted, in the back yard in a washtub full of water warmed by the sun. The children had assigned chores, a very important part of family life in those days. According to Pete, "On wash day we knew to stay out of the way!" Fan (as his mother was called) and the girls, Jo and Grace, the third and fourth children, "did not want any distraction or foolishness while they had the wash pots on the fire in the front yard." The girls cleaned the glass lamp chimneys in the house and the boys cut and brought in firewood. Tobe (James Donald), the second oldest, kept the homemade kindling box, near the sink, full of pine fatwood. He slit the logs thinly so they would ignite quickly and, too, it made the load last longer. The children sometimes took a piece of burning wood and buried it in a shallow hole to make charcoal. The ladies, who did all the cooking, knew how to keep the stove hot and where to put things on the top to vary the temperature of the items cooking. The back burners were usually not as hot as the front burners, but would keep things warm or simmering until needed.

Pete's oldest brother, Carl, the first born in the family, would sleep across the road at his maternal Aunt Bula's house when Uncle John Phillips was gone, making more sleeping room at the Turnham house. Once, when Pete had not really had enough to eat, he went to Aunt Bula's house and was milling around when Aunt Bula said, "There's a sweet potato left in the oven if you want it." Aunt Bula

1924 - STANDING LEFT TO RIGHT
GRACE, CARL, TOBE, JO
SITTING: HENRY, PETE, AND FAN

kept a bowl of sweet potatoes on the table and would say, "Leave those alone. They're Pete's!" to anyone who tried to take one. Not surprisingly, according to Pete, "Aunt Bula loved me and I loved her!" And, Pete and his Aunt Bula shared a middle name, Benton. Another time, when Pete was older, the family had not had meat for three days. Pete, remembering where a rabbit hole was, took his gun and killed the rabbit for supper. Family love and helpfulness abounded.

The Turnhams, of English descent, were farmers and mill workers and had lived in the area for generations. Some would have said they were poor, but in that area, and particularly after the Great Depression hit at the end of 1929, the children never realized they

14

were poor because they had a roof over their heads, food to eat, all their neighbors and classmates lived much like they did, and, above all, they knew they were loved by their parents and extended family. Pete has said, "My parents had six kids. We lived in a four-room house and ate what we grew. We didn't know we were poor. Everybody was in the same fix. Life was hard, real hard. But, it was hard for everybody."

Another sign of the times, so common in those days, was when children got a pair of shoes their parents told them the shoes had to last a year. Pete's one-armed Uncle Boach, who lived near them, stretched that scenario a little further with his four kids. Back then, Sears and Roebuck stores had a policy that if

TURNHAM HOME IN ABANDA

the shoes tore up you could get a new pair free. According to Pete, "They'd let one kid wear them, then the next one. They were rough on them in that red dirt. When the shoes wore out they'd just send them in for a new pair!" To Pete's chagrin, he said Sears would send them a new pair from Atlanta within a few days and even pay the postage. On a visit to see another uncle, Tom Sessions, who lived in Atlanta, Pete told him there was one thing he wanted to see, and that was Sears Roebuck. "He took me and that was the biggest store I ever saw!"

A precocious child, Pete was curious and a thinker. As a toddler, his curiosity took him too near the fireplace, his clothes caught fire and his stomach was burned, leaving permanent scar tissue. The scars almost kept him out of the army, but when Pete said it did not keep him from doing anything he wanted to do he was accepted. He had a bit of a stubborn streak, and this trait once caused his sister, Jo, as well as himself, a moment neither of them would forget. "When I was not too big I was out in the back yard playing with Grace and Jo (sisters) and Mama hollered to me out the back screen door to do something and I wouldn't do it. She was really mad. She came out to punish me, and we

PETE - AGE 4

could tell it was going to be a bad one. Jo said, 'Don't spank him!' Mama was fuming and asked, 'Do YOU want to take it?,' and she did." Years later she recalled that it was

15

one of the worst whippings she ever got, and it was probably one of the reasons Pete always loved her so dearly.

As a first grader, while playing ball, Pete ran down a bank to get the ball, fell, and broke his right arm. The break was so bad the bone was sticking out of his inner-forearm. "My teacher, Mrs. Floy Roton, picked me up in her arms and carried me to Dr. Thomas Clack's office about a quarter mile or more away." Dr. Clack, blinded by a hemorrhage only three years after he began practicing medicine, continued to practice with his wife, Thresia, becoming his "eyes". She stayed close by his side, driving him all over Chambers County, relating his patients' symptoms, and then, for long hours at home, reading medical journals to him. With great admiration, Pete said, "He set my arm and I never had a minute's trouble out of it."

Pete's favorite activities as a youngster were fishing and hunting. He also enjoyed playing baseball on a converted football field by the school. As the two youngest, he and Bill begged Carl and Tobe and their older friends to let them play baseball with them in a cow pasture behind Abanda Baptist Church. He played basketball at Milltown High which had an outdoor court measured off on hard dirt. "We didn't know anything about politics then and we thought everybody was like us." The money for school sports came from the size of the school's enrollment and Pete said, "The money was just not there" for a gym or inside court. In those days they played Union Hill on their outdoor court and Wadley and Lafayette on their inside courts. Though limited by his size, Pete said he had fun playing. Memories of those early years also included a special childhood game he, his siblings, and his neighbors played. They lived on a hill and would gather on the hill at night, watch the car lights on the road, and pretend they were watching a movie.

By the time Pete was 14, his dad had managed to buy a little more property. From

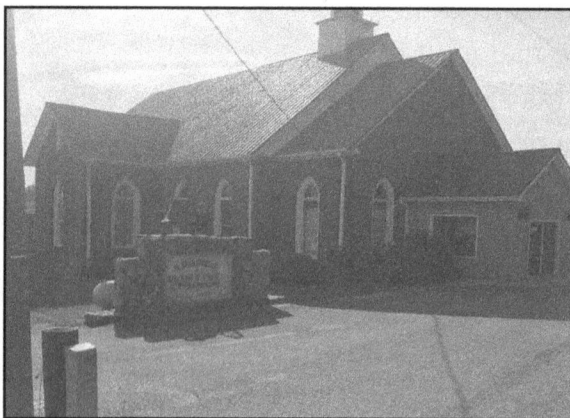

ABANDA BAPTIST CHURCH

the back of a mule, Pete managed a crew of workers in those fields, another sign he was destined to be a hard worker and a leader. Many of the workers were older than Pete and he said, "I worked hard to stay ahead of them so they'd work hard."

A special memory was when Robert Langford, the preacher at Abanda Baptist Church, invited Henry Allen Parker, then at Howard College (now Samford University), to preach at a revival in 1936. The Turnham boys were hoeing at Katy Creek with their daddy. It was extremely hot, and their daddy told them they could stop hoeing if they would go to church. Pete said, "Boy, we dropped our hoes and left right then! We got all cleaned up and headed out." Pete remembered Henry Allen "was a real good preacher, he was good looking, and he had a real good presentation." It was that night, at the age of 15, when Pete joined the church. Many years later when Henry Allen was serving a church in Montgomery, Pete went by to see him and tell him about his memories of that special night. Pete said another sweet memory was of often hearing his mother sing hymns as she came up the dirt driveway from the barn with a pail in her hands. The family worshiped at the Abanda Baptist Church down the road, and baptisms were done nearby in the creek. To this day, Pete loves that church.

PETE GROOMING CALF

CALF PETE GROOMED PLACED
FIRST IN SHOW

As a teen, Pete became very active in the 4-H Club and in The Future Farmers of America. He would hang around the office of the FFA leader, Ernest L. Stewart, lean on the doorway, and tell stories and jokes. E. L. had a good calf and was so impressed with Pete he asked him if he would like to groom the calf and place him in a show in LaFayette. Pete grabbed the opportunity and that calf won first place, an early indication of his abilities, tenacity, and ambitions. Pete became the state FFA treasurer in 1937 and twice he traveled by train to the national FFA convention in Kansas City, Missouri. In order to pay for the trips Mr. Stewart helped him with fund-raisers in Milltown. Attending the four-day convention and paying for his room and meals cost $25, a lot of money in those days. On one of the trips home Pete met a young man from Birmingham and got off the train with him. As the train was pulling into Birmingham he had seen a sign advertising shoes for $5.00, so he walked into town along the railroad tracks and bought a pair. In order to purchase the shoes he had to take the money out of what he had left. He said, "I did without some food to get shoes. I had two candy bars that day." Pete had to be back at the station by 3:00 PM in order to catch the last train to Abanda, which arrived at 8:00 PM. When the train arrived, Pete said, "Everybody met me at the railroad station. We celebrated! I showed them all my

FFA OFFICERS,
PETE, SECOND FROM RIGHT

new shoes!" On the trip he made as a senior, on October 18, 1938, Pete was one of three young Alabama farmers elected to the degree of "American Farmer".

A few teachers, especially in the harder courses, took a special interest in Pete. One day Miss Celia Cumbie, one of those special teachers, told him to stay a little later after class because she wanted to talk with him about something. She wanted to talk to him about going to Alabama Polytechnic Institute and she said he had to learn to write essays to go there. She gave him four or five subjects and he wrote essays on each one. According to Pete, "That was a routine I got into. I was going to school full time, writing essays, and working on the farm. It wasn't easy."

Pete's mother's sister, Nettye, her husband, Vird Findley, and their adored only child, Jack, lived in Lanett where Vird worked in the cotton mill. Every Friday the family would drive to Abanda and return to Lanett on Sunday. Pete said he worshiped Vird because Vird would do little things for him and "there were so many of us we had to do for our own selves." On one of their visits, as Pete and Jack were approaching high school graduation, several in the Sessions family were sitting on the front porch of Pete's house. The subject of college came up and someone asked the boys what they were going to do. His Aunt Nett said, "We're going to send Jack to Auburn", and she told how they would do it. After everyone bragged on Jack, Aunt Nett said, "Well, Pete, you haven't said what you're going to do." Pete said he was going to Auburn, too. Aunt Nett laughed and said, "I'll tell you this, you'll never go to Auburn, because we're having to move down there, get a place to live, get a job, and work during the week." Pete said listening to all she had to say about him not being able to go to Auburn made him more determined.

Leaving Home

The founder of the town of Auburn was Judge John J. Harper of Harris County, Georgia. He led a group of settlers there in late 1836, soon after the forced removal from east Alabama of the last Native Americans, remnants of the Creek nation. Judge Harper was largely responsible for the establishment of the Auburn Methodist Church. Though other denominations soon followed, the Methodists had an important influence on the early history of the village, particularly establishing educational institutions. Judge Harper's half-brother, Nathaniel Scott, led the movement to establish the Auburn Masonic Female College, which opened in 1853, and Scott and the Reverend John Bowles Glenn encouraged the local congregation to establish the East Alabama Male College, a Methodist institution that began classes in 1859 and served as the forerunner of Auburn University. The Civil War, 1861 to 1865, devastated Auburn, leaving the community and the college destitute, and local commerce and staple crop agriculture in ruins with no source of credit to provide funds to start over. The state took over the impoverished Methodist College in 1872 and the name was changed to the Agricultural and Mechanical College, but for many years the state provided no annual appropriations to run it. By 1888, however, the college and the town showed a few signs of returning to prosperity. In 1899 the name of the college became Alabama Polytechnic Institute. By 1907 the enrollment at the college reached 600, which, at the time, made it the largest student body in Alabama. The Great Depression of 1929 lasted for more than a decade in Auburn, but New Deal programs contributed importantly to the construction of buildings on campus.

When Pete graduated from Chambers County High School in Milltown on May 22, 1939, the Civilian Conservation Corps was in full operation all over the country.

This was part of President Franklin Roosevelt's "New Deal", which operated from 1933 to 1942 for young men ages 17 to 28, to provide unskilled manual labor jobs related to the conservation and development of natural resources in rural lands owned by federal, state, and local governments. This helped young men find work and help their families still struggling from the Great Depression. Maximum enrollment was 300,000 nation-wide. It provided shelter, clothing, and food, and Pete said, "They paid $30 per month. You had to send $22 home and keep $8, for toothpaste and such." Pete went to the LaFayette courthouse to find out about the CCC, was told who to see, and signed up, on July 6th. He said, "I had a shirt, a change of underwear, and maybe a quarter, and they scheduled four or five of us to leave at four o'clock that afternoon for Auburn." Someone in the Welfare Department drove them the forty miles south to their assignment, Chewacla State Park, where construction had begun in September 1935 and was completed in March 1941. Pete began with road building duty working with a pick, a shovel, and his hands. Soon after his arrival, he said it hit him that he definitely needed to get an education. From that position he was assigned to run the camp canteen and later became a night watchman, which allowed him to attend classes at API during the day. The men were issued clothes similar to Army uniforms, khakis for summer and heavy greens for winter. They were fed three plain but good meals a day and built solid muscle from the hard manual labor. Pete arrived at a weight of 115 pounds and left two years later weighing 135 pounds. He said, "It was tough and it made us tough." Work done by the CCC at Chewacla included building the dam and 26 acre lake, cabins, manager's house, pavilions, bridges, roads, and hiking trails.

Typically looking to enhance any situation, Pete said, "They had a church service for us, and my friend and I helped organize a Sunday school. We tried to get a preacher to come out to the camp and preach, and when they couldn't do it, we tried to get them to come out and take us into town to the church." While at Chewacla, Pete became friends with Forrest Lee Mathews, the education director of the camp. They raised chickens and hogs and the two of them helped the men working with them learn to read, write, and master agriculture skills. Forest Lee's father was the superintendent of schools in Grove Hill; and, years later, when Pete was traveling in the southwest Alabama area, he would stay with Mr. Matthews and his wife. They fixed up a little room for him and called it "Pete's room." When Forrest Lee, who also became a school superintendent, had a son, David, the elder Mr. Mathews told Pete he "was going to have to send David (his grandson) to Auburn for a year or two to get him polished up." David Mathews later became president of the University of Alabama.

The CCC facilities at Chewacla formed the first state park infrastructure in the state of Alabama. Pete later said, "organization and operation of CCC camps as a military organization served the United States well when war came." Receiving an honorable discharge from the CCC on June 30, 1941, with his "manner of performance" rated excellent, Pete, an alumnus of Company 4448, SP-12, gave the invocation at the dedication of the historical marker for Chewacla State Park on October 25, 2009.

While working for the CCC, Pete began night classes at Auburn (then Alabama Polytechnic Institute) with an emphasis in chemistry. He also became a member of the required ROTC program. The campus was six miles from Chewalca, and to get to classes Pete bought a bicycle. He hitch-hiked a ride to Humphrey Tire and Auto Company in Opelika and bought a bicycle for a dollar and a quarter down and a dollar and a quarter a month. He also had to pay for a chain and lock.

COLLEGE ANNUAL PICTURE

When the CCC program ended, Pete moved to a boarding house and got another job. "We had a commissary in the ROTC in Auburn and it was in the recreation hall. They had an opening. I got the job. It paid $32 a month, and I sent $8 home to the family each month. That was the cash flow I had." Tuition at Auburn was $45 a semester.

ROTC ARTILLERY TRAINING -
PETE 2ND FROM RIGHT

Because it was a land grant college, the first two years of ROTC were required for every man enrolled at Auburn. For the next two years advanced ROTC was optional, but there was a small stipend for those who continued. Pete said he stayed in the program so he could stay in school. One could choose his area of study and he chose artillery, 105 millimeter. The first sergeant he saw when he began ROTC

21

COLLEGE DAYS

liked to play ping-pong, and he beat everybody in the camp. Pete played ping-pong with anybody who would play him, learned to play well, and beat the sergeant. This made the sergeant "friendly mad" and Pete happy, another example of Pete's drive to excel. Always a doer, while a student at Auburn, Pete was an active member of the Baptist Student Union, the Agriculture Club, was tapped into Gamma Sigma Delta Honor Society of Agriculture, and was a Sears Scholar, receiving a $100 scholarship from Sears Roebuck and Company awarded to some of the students in the School of Agriculture. He pledged Alpha Gamma Rho Fraternity and later became its president.

"Every four or five months my mother and daddy would get somebody to bring them down to Auburn to see me. We had a real close relationship," Pete said. Proudly, his parents were present when he graduated from API in August of 1944 with a degree in Animal Husbandry.

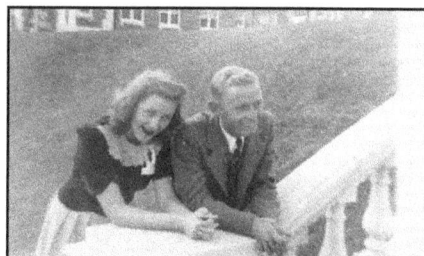
1942 KAY AND PETE
COLLEGE SWEETHEARTS

Ping-pong continued to play an important role in Pete's life when he met Nettye Kathryn "Kay" Rice while playing ping-pong in the basement recreation room of Auburn First Baptist Church. "I teased her. I let her beat me so she'd be nice to me," said Pete. They dated for a couple of years before marrying on August 25, 1943, at Inglenook Baptist Church in Birmingham, and honeymooning at Cheaha State Park 78 miles north of Auburn. Pete said they were friends first then fell in love, saying, "Back then you married for

KAY AND PETE MARRIED
AUGUST 25, 1943

NEWLYWEDS

love". An early test of their young marriage was when Pete left for WWII as an Army platoon leader.

The War Years

1944

*F*ollowing graduation, Pete immediately went into active military duty. He said, "We believed in serving our country. We begged them to let us go right then. And, they did." Pete was included in a train-load of Auburn advanced ROTC students who had been taken to Ft. McPherson, Georgia for training in April 1942, where they were sworn in on June 17th. After graduation from API in August 1944, Pete trained with the 342nd Armored Field Artillery Battalion at Ft. Sill, Oklahoma. He then went to Fort Benning in Columbus, Georgia for basic training where, after completing the Officer Candidate Course at The Infantry School, he was officially sworn into active duty on October 3, 1944. Having been a private from April 1943 and a Corporal from March 1944, Pete was commissioned a second lieutenant and put in charge of 42 men. Kay went to Columbus to tell him good-bye, and in January 1945 he went to New York to board one of several troop ships bound for Austria. At the age of 96 and with tears in his eyes once again, Pete said, "I remember when I passed the Statue of Liberty I felt something on my cheeks. I reached up and it was tears. I thought, 'I wonder if I'll ever see you again?' And I remember when I came back and saw her I said, 'We made it!'" According to Pete, several times during the seven-day voyage the ships stopped and everyone wondered why. They later learned that there were German submarines in sight. When Pete arrived in Austria he said it was the coldest he had ever been in his life.

After a two or three day layover, the ship docked in Le Havre, France, where Pete had an interesting experience. "I was in training at Ft. Benning with John Eisenhower and often went into town (Columbus) with him. He had access to a vehicle and money to buy gas. His father, Dwight Eisenhower, was the commander of the American forces. When we got to Le Havre, we started unloading and a little tugboat came up beside the ship. Over the loud speaker they called for Lt. John Eisenhower, the same one I knew. Somebody I was standing near said, 'I wonder where he is?' I said, 'Reading the Stars and Stripes.' You get more out of the Stars and Stripes than you do from the New York Times!" Pete says people often ask him why he reads so much history and he says, "Tradition! Tradition is a tremendous asset. We have tradition because we have values. We break those values sometimes not even realizing it. But you have to move on."

Made the day before we crossed Danube on April 25, 1945. This was over rear assembly area. We went to bed + was awoke at one A.M. with orders to move. We marched from then until the next day at 11 A.M. It seemed more than any human could stand in rain + mud, but I had you to carry me on.

In April 1945 Pete wrote on the back of a picture he sent home to Kay, "…we crossed Danube on April 25, 1945. We went to bed and were awoken at one AM with orders to move. We marched from then until the next day at 11 AM. It seemed more than any human could stand in rain and mud, but I had you to carry me on." On the back of a picture of Pete and another man in his unit, Sgt. "Stump Jumpin'" Johnson, cooking on a small squad heater he wrote, "The meal consisted of 1 can of pork and beans, a few pieces of candy, and some crackers. We were here protecting the flank of the battalion." Another photo back said, "During the war the men got tired from long marches, no sleep, poor food. Note the heavy packs." Still another, a picture of some of the men under his command, said, "The gallant group of men I had the privilege of leading in combat. Notice how tired, but yet determined, they look. Here you see a cross

Sgt. Johnson (Stump Jumpin') and me cooking our supper on a small squad heater. The meal consisted of 1 can of pork + beans, a few pieces of candy and some crackers. We were here protecting the flank of the battalion. My C.P. was just inside the woods. Taken in April.

The gallant group of men I had the privilege of leading in combat. Notice how tired, but yet determined, they look. Here you see a cross section of America — the men who will make sure our country never goes to war again — we hope. Made in April

section of America – the men who will make sure our country never goes to war again – we hope."

After moving into Saarbruken, Germany, on the back of another picture Pete wrote, "A bombed out street in Saarbruken, Germany, taken June, 1945. The entire city was just like this and where the people were living I didn't know. This is one of the most badly bombed towns I've seen. War is awful!" As the Allies continued to move forward Pete said, "Hitler was getting desperate. He was having youth camps and bringing teenagers in there for training."

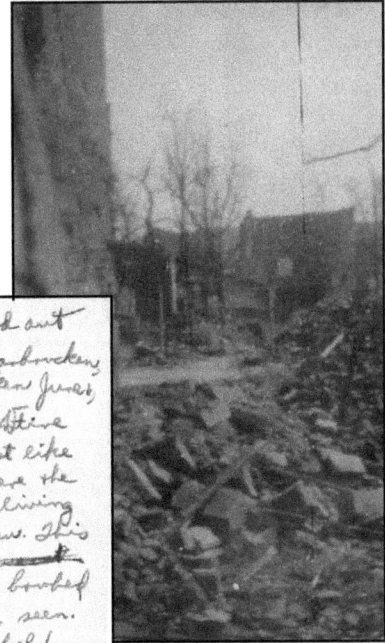

a bombed out street in Saarbruken, Germany, taken June, 1945. The entire city was just like this and where the people were living I didn't know. This is one of the most badly bombed towns I've seen. War is awful!

On a picture made in November he wrote, " 'I will lift up mine eyes unto the hills' is the second thing I thought of after seeing this. You, of course, were my first thought. I was on a rather high hill looking back toward these snow covered peaks. Fussen –Markt – Oberdorf road. Nov. 1945."

1945 PETE WITH RUSSIAN CHILDREN

My Russian Buddies & I (you probably have one or more like this)

In July of 1945 Pete's battalion was in Paris, France. Always seeking opportunities, Pete enrolled at the University of Paris and took a course in agriculture. Earlier, on February 20th, he had written a letter to Dr. C.L. Isbell, one of his professors at Auburn in the Horticulture and Forestry department.

25

Somewhere in France

Dear Dr. Isbell,

After moving around over France for several days I have at last become stationed in my new home. It's one of these types you read about with mud about 8 inches deep serving as the carpet. I'm not grumbling though, for millions of others are doing the same thing.

No doubt you have started your spring gardening orchard work and many new experiments, as I'm certain Auburn is enjoying the budding of spring.

Recently I was reading an article on vitamin C content of tomatoes and it stated some varieties were not very high in the content. Do our leading varieties in Ala. such as Burbank, Marglobe and the others contain a large amount? I believe they do but would like to know from you. If I remember correctly Ponderosa is rather high in vitamin C.

Due to military regulations they won't let us write of the farming in France. However, I'm not too impressed over their methods. I'll take the worn out soil of the South any day. One at least enjoys improving its fertility.

Haven't found any Auburn boys yet but would really welcome the sight of them. I need some help to yell "War Eagle" as my voice alone won't carry too well.

Sincerely,
Pete B. Turnham

Joe, Pete's son, says Pete's all-time favorite picture is of General George S. Patton in a jeep addressing the Third Army, of which Pete was a part. According to Joe, "George Patton named his Jeep the War Eagle. Patton was at Fort Benning and he used to watch the Auburn vs. Georgia games in Colum-

GEN. GEORGE PATTON IN "WAR EAGLE" JEEP

bus, Georgia where they were played at that time. Patton admired the way the Auburn team fought so much he wanted his men to fight like the War Eagles did, so he named his Jeep the War Eagle! Dad has had more fun making copies of that picture and sending it to people."

CREMATORIUM

Under the command of General George S. Patton, First Lieutenant Turnham fought on the front lines in France, Germany, and Austria. His unit continued to grow and by the end of the war the 24-year-old was leading a 200-man infantry company. On May 4, 1945, his infantry division, the 71st, liberated Gunskirchen Lager near Lambach, one of the many sub-camps of the Mauthausen concentration camp in Austria. In addition to

400 political prisoners, some 17,000 Hungarian Jews reportedly passed through the camp. When the 71st entered the camp, about 15,000 prisoners were still there. In the months following, some 1,500 former prisoners died from typhus, dysentery, and as a consequence of mistreatment by the Nazis. According to Tim, Pete's son, Pete told him that, as a young officer, he didn't really know what the war was about. But when he witnessed the liberation of Gunskirchen Lager, with all the inhumane conditions and atrocities there, he knew. "We were in there first, so we saw the horrors before anybody else did. You talk about skin and bones. It just makes you cry. Some of them tried to come to us and just dropped dead, they were so exhausted. You see such as this and you know why you fight in a war. It's all about humans and democracy. I wouldn't have believed this if I hadn't seen it." Major General Willard G. Wyman, Commanding Officer, wrote a booklet about Gunskirchen Lager and in the forward he said, "The damning evidence against the Nazi war criminals found at Gunskirchen Lager is being recorded in this booklet in the hope that the lessons learned in Germany will not soon be forgotten by the democratic nations of the individual men who fought to wipe out a government built on hate, greed, race myths and murder. The horror of Gunskirchen must not be repeated." Pete sent a copy of the booklet home to Kay and in the inside cover he wrote the following:

> *"December 6, 1945 – To those who read this sickening account there should be no doubt left as to why Americans came abroad to fight in World War II. I witnessed this sight and will never forget the horrors. One morning as I was issuing the days rations to my men, some of these starving prisoners were standing nearby and grabbed for every bite of food they saw. Some would grasp the food and drop dead from hunger before they could take a bite. There was nothing halfway decent around the place – another case where the Germans tried to show their brutality by starving innocent people. Let us hope that such will never again take place.*
>
> *Pete B. Turnham, 2nd Lt. Infantry."*

While on occupation duty, Pete said he was assigned as director of a prison camp in Bavaria. It was his duty to supervise the hanging of a German farmer convicted of killing a downed American airman with a pitchfork. "That, too, was a scene I shall not forget. The condemned man, who could speak some English, prayed gently and softly for forgiveness before the trap was sprung".

In April 1945, during fighting near a little village in Germany named Hartenstein, Pete and another lieutenant got under a half-tent and plotted a barrage, a barrier of artillery fire laid on a line close to friendly troops to screen and protect them. The next morning, as they began the barrage, the enemy pinned Pete's men down with heavy fire supported by tanks. But, by firing white phosphorus back at them, Pete said, "That was enough to stop them." The next week Pete received the Bronze Star medal with a "V" for valor demonstrating bravery and heroism against an enemy force during combat. The official document stated:

First Lieutenant Pete B. Turnham (then Second Lieutenant), Infantry Company C, 66th Infantry Regiment, United States Army. For heroic achievement in connection with military operations against an enemy of the United States in Germany. On 21 April 1945, Lieutenant Turnham was directing his platoon in defense of hill positions near Hartenstein, Germany, when the enemy launched a vicious attack supported by tanks. With his platoon caught in a wedge between the attacking infantry and tank units, Lieutenant Turnham repeatedly exposed himself to enemy rifle and automatic weapons fire in order to place his men in advantageous positions and effectively direct the defense. He personally led two rocket launcher teams in the face of the attacking tanks. With fearless disregard for his personal safety, he exposed himself to intense enemy fire to direct accurate rocket fire which destroyed one tank, disabled two others, and forced the enemy to withdraw with heavy casualties. His outstanding aggressive leadership, courage, and loyal devotion to duty reflect high credit upon himself and the military service.

Also, close to the end of the war near Fussen, Germany, at the Austrian border, Pete's unit was trapped on the edge of a potato field. Pete said, "They taught you in war when you were being shot at to run a few feet and drop, run again and drop." Using this technique, all his men made it to the woods on the other side of the field. Then Pete ran across the field in the same manner, and his men laughed and teased him when he reached them. Pete said, "The men were probably glad I made it, and

Mr. Pete

it was probably like a funny training film to watch me cross alone, up and running and down to the ground. And, the laughter released tension, too."

One of Pete's friends from high school, Robert Horn, wrote to Pete while he was in the war. Robert was an assistant County Agent in Chambers County and very active with the 4-H Club when writing to Pete. Just after VE (Victory in Europe) Day, Pete sent a letter to Robert.

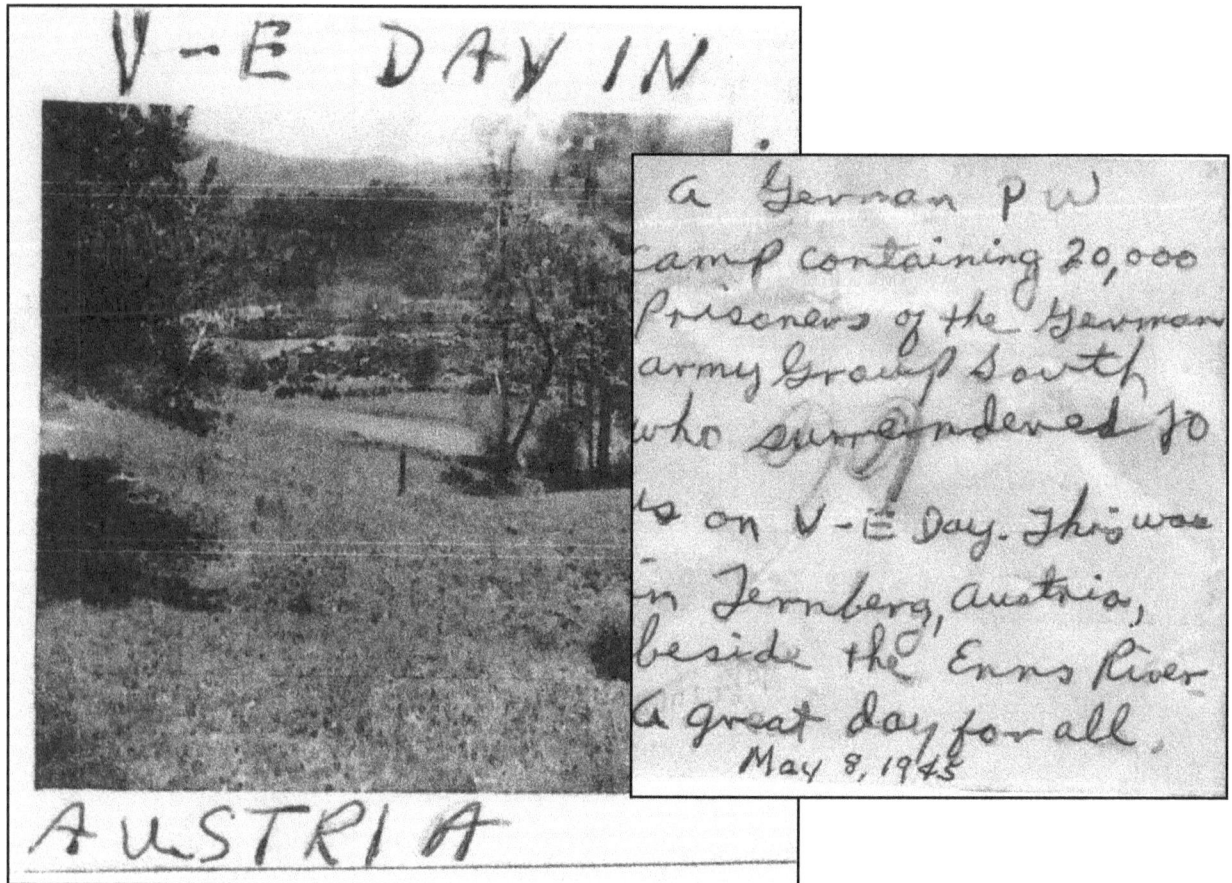

V-E DAY IN AUSTRIA

a German PW camp containing 20,000 prisoners of the German army Group South who surrendered to us on V-E Day. This was in Fernberg, Austria, beside the Enns River a great day for all.
May 8, 1945

May 11, 1945

Dear R.C.,

Your letter of April 26 came three days ago — V-E Day. You wished the war would be over when I received it, and surely enough that was the case. I'm keeping the letter in my billfold for good luck.

The 4-H Rally must have been wonderful! It seems only yesterday when I stood on the stage and presided over the best group of clubs in all of

30

Alabama – at least I thought so. Boys and girls get so much good from meetings like that. ......

The weather is very delightful here in Austria, but it's probably due to the fact that we're in a mountainous area – snow still covers the highest peaks. In the valley below flows the swift, clear Inns River. I'm near Wels, Austria.

For the past several days we have received some twenty thousand Germans that came in to surrender in our sector. I've wondered how long it would have taken us to dig them out with bayonets. The German army is truly beaten. Their vehicles are worn out; their guns are old and inferior to ours; their men are so old (2/3 of them) until I wonder why God allowed the war to last this long. Yet, on the other hand, some of their men are fifteen and sixteen. It's only a miracle they lasted this long.

Our outfit is taking its first rest since back in February, but had we stopped before the end, the Germans would have dug in and we would have lost more men than we did in breaking their defense line. Many of my men are in hospitals now as a result of over-working. Frankly, I'm run down, and my men say I look ten years older – That was before I got a shower, haircut and shave though.

Give Mr. J.W. Drake my best regards. He's one of the finest men I've ever known. During my days in the C.C.C. he was a constant companion and advisor, and he offered me a few suggestions that helped tremendously toward getting through college. His family is one of the best I've ever known. Tell him it wouldn't take much to beat me in tennis now, but that wasn't hard to do back in '39 & '40. He's a good tennis player.

Last week Kenneth Funchess and I got together for about four hours and cooked a big meal of ham and chicken. (Don't ask me where we got it though) He flies a liaison plane for the 71st Division. That's the first Auburn man I've seen over here yet. .....

Kay likes her job at St. Margaret's in Montgomery but says she's working awful hard. Drop by to see her if you are down that way soon.

31

I'm wondering if they will need me in the Pacific theater now. Though I'd rather come home, I'll gladly go and help defeat the "rats" of the East. The heat over there must be awful.

Among my collections of war "booty" I have a German Luger pistol, one P-38, an Austrian 38, one Belgium 32 and a Czech. 38. I'm planning to bring the luger and P-38 home, as I had the happy privilege of taking them from two Germans myself.

Everyday I think what a wonderful job you are doing there in 4-H club work. Our youth needs a leader like you, and I feel certain they are being guided the right way under you. Looking back to my days as a 4-H member (and I'm still one I hope) I well remember how much my 4-H and F.F.A. advisors meant to me. By the way, do you ever see Mr. E.L. Stewart? He's at Tuskegee now with the 4-H work.

A letter from Dr. Isbell at Auburn indicated that school was rather short of students now. He stated that Harry was due home soon, since he had completed his missions with the 8th air force.

Hope you stay well and happy and that your work will continue to progress in every way. I feel certain it will.

Sincerely your friend,
Pete

Thinking they would be heading home soon after victory in Europe, May 8, 1945, Pete's unit, instead, began training in light tank combat, preparing to fight in Japan, when they were diverted and sent to Bavaria, near Germany's border with Austria, to guard the Newschwanstein Castle (the inspiration for the castle in Disneyland) and its contents. The men spent the summer and fall of 1945 in a hotel at the foot of the castle guarding the thousands of pieces of art, mostly from France, hidden there. The Nazis had stolen the art and Hitler had planned to put it in a museum after the war. The Monuments Men, a popular movie about the rescue of those pieces of art, was made in 2014. Pete said most of the art was packed and crated and he had no idea how valuable it was. Only later, after he learned the art's value, did he realize what he had been protecting.

Schloß Neuschwanstein mit Hohenschwangau

Lt. Pete B. Ivenham 0-927072
Co. "C" 66th Inf. A.P.O. 360
C/O P.M. N.Y., N.Y.
          Fussen, Germany
          Oct. 16, 1945

Honey,
    This is the castle
I wrote you about
visiting. It is a mile
from our hotel, which
is the one marked x
below the castle.
        I love you —
                Hubby

Nr. 748

Martin Herpich & Sohn, Kunst- u. Verlagsanstalt

Mrs. Pete B. Ivenham
3503 Vanderbilt Rd.
Birmingham 7, Ala.

Free

U.S. ARMY 360 OCT 18 1945 POSTAL SERVICE

33

PETE'S JEEP AT KAY'S PARENTS' GAS STATION IN BIRMINGHAM

In December 1945 Pete was promoted to First Lieutenant. Knowing he would need transportation when he got home, Pete had the opportunity to buy an army ¼ ton 4 X 4 Jeep, number 78, under the Surplus Property Act of 1944. He made the purchase on May 16, 1946, and arrangements were made to ship it to New York on the USAT Henry Gibbons, arriving July 2nd.

On June 9, 1946, Pete boarded a ship from La Havre, France, to New York City, arriving June 20th after fighting and being in war torn Europe for a year and a half. Many years after the war Pete said, "The Germans were glad the war was over. They were dedicated, good people who had been misled by a bad leader."

On August 16, 1946, Pete was officially separated from active duty in the Army of the United States. The description of his service read as follows:

Infantry Platoon leader from 2 October, 1944 to July, 1945. Responsible for security, care and feeding of forty-one men in combat. August to October, 1945 was Liaison Officer for displaced persons, representing the 1st Battalion, 66 Infantry, responsible to 71st Division, Commanding General. October, 1945 to March, 1946 was Company Commander of Company C, 66th Infantry, responsible for security, welfare and feeding and training of one hundred and eighty five men and five officers. Became Executive Officer of light tank troop, 14th Constabulary Regiment in March to the end of May. Responsible for food, fuel, and medical supplies and general welfare of five thousand displaced Russians, Ukrainians and Poles. In charge of internal security of Landsberg Prison, prison where Dachan criminals were being held prior to execution.

PETE, TOBE
AND BILL

Three Brothers In Service

After his time of active duty Pete stayed in the Army Reserves and continued to progress in rank. In July 1950 he attained the rank of Captain in Army Intelligence, completing all four phases of 3AA MI School, progressing from Executive Officer to Company Commander. Some of the comments on his evaluation sheets were: "Capt. Turnham has participated in reserve program very actively and effectively. Appears to be far above average in intelligence and is mentally and physically alert. Officer possesses unusual energy and imagination. Thoroughly honest and dependable." After serving for 20 years, Pete retired as a Major.

ALL SAFELY BACK HOME. L TO R:
MR. HENRY, JO, CARL, FAN, TOBE, GRACE, PETE, AND BILL

A proud moment for Pete was when he was recognized as the Distinguished Veteran of the Year by the Auburn Veterans Committee and was presented a commemorative flag at the ceremony on April 5, 2009.

Getting Established
and Making a Home

Kay had been living in a dormitory on campus at Auburn when Pete returned to the states from the war. She found a one-room apartment for them on Samford Avenue in the home of an Auburn professor, Dave Bottoms, and his wife, Margaret. Pete remembers the couple had two sons and the family was very nice to them. Kay had finished her degree in Laboratory Technology, had worked at St. Margaret's Hospital in Montgomery, at Physician's Medical Laboratory Service in Sarasota, Florida, and at several research labs at Alabama Polytechnic Institute. She continued working at the university and for the next two years, and with the GI Bill and his salary from the Army Reserves, Pete resumed his studies at API, completing an MS in Artificial Breeding and Herd Improvement in 1948.

Upon graduation, Pete went to work as an assistant extension dairy specialist with the Alabama Cooperative Extension System, through API, in charge of dairy herd improvement. Working with Alabama dairymen, he set up two statewide programs, dairying and artificial breeding. He completed an intensive study of the Dairy Herd Improvement Association at the University of Georgia, at that time one of the leading promoters in the field, and also did course work at Penn State College under Professor C. R. Gearhart, then the nation's most noted authority on D.H.I.A. work. Speaking to recently elected officers of the Chambers County 4-H Club, Pete said one of the things he valued most was the association he had with other boys and girls in competing for showmanship when his calf won first place in the junior division in 1938. He said, "You are on the right road to a greater calf club program for 4-H members in Chambers County. I noticed this year that there was keen competition among junior showmen. We must always keep in mind the ideal cow and breed toward that. My opinion is that what success we have made in dairying during the past decade in the South has been in feeding and management, and not breeding. Of course, some progress has been made in breeding, but less than 10 sires were proved in Alabama last year. We need to place a great deal of emphasis on breeding, feeding, and weeding." Under Pete's leadership, the D.H.I.A. was initially set up in five Alabama counties, and gradually encompassed the entire state. Each association hired a supervisor who would test milk, keep records of weights and productions, and check feed accounts. Those supervisors would assist farmers in determining which cows were most profitable in their herds and which should be sold. Pete, working through county agents, helped the farmers set up their associations and assisted them by working with testers, and by passing on other information concerning the functioning of such associations. He also directed the training programs at API for those supervisors. Another milestone through Pete's work was the first calf conceived by artificial insemination in Alabama. The D.H.I.A. program continued and Pete received a commendation for never losing any of the sites throughout the state. Dr. W.H. Eaton, one of Pete's professors, taught his students a poem and Pete still enjoys quoting it today.

The Dairy cow is a thing of charm,
She lifts the mortgage from the farm.
She makes the farmer's life more sweet,
And puts him down on easy street.

Near the end of his tenure with API, as toastmaster of the Alabama Dairy Herd Improvement banquet at the university, Pete impressed everyone by being able to call almost all of the 200 persons present by their first names, another indication he was headed for a life of public service.

AERIAL VIEW OF
GRAVES CENTER APARTMENTS

Pete and Kay moved into an apartment in married student housing, Graves Center Apartments, what had previously been military bunkers, and on June 8, 1948, they welcomed their first child, a beautiful baby girl, Diane Dale. At that time there were no obstetricians in Auburn, so they had to drive to Montgomery for pre-natal care and for Diane's birth at St. Margaret's hospital. Also, there was no maternity insurance available, so the money had to be saved and paid when the baby was born. Pete remembered this as he later worked in the legislature to make things better. Soon after Pete became a legislator, a Mrs. Moreman, who owned a restaurant in Opelika, approached Pete and said a good hospital was needed there and she wanted him to get a bill passed for a 2 mil county tax rate just for that purpose. The bill passed and Lee County

FOUR GENERATIONS
SALLY, J. HENRY, PETE, AND DIANE

Hospital, now East Alabama Medical Center (EAMC) was built. EAMC, now a nationally respected regional health care facility, is still getting money from the tax today, still helping those patients who cannot pay their full bill. It's the second largest employer in the county, Auburn University being the first. When Kay was a patient in EAMC in June 2009, Pete and Diane were in the cafeteria and Pete told Diane there was a lesson to be learned from the story. "One woman sparked a wonderful thing which is bearing rich fruit for the region. Dream and get help from key people to fulfill it. One man showed diligence in serving his community, and his own wife is benefiting from it now in room 5123."

DIANE TURNHAM

With the impending arrival of their second child in 1950, more room was needed for the growing family. Pete bought a couple of acres on

PETE, DIANE, AND TIM

Moore's Mill Road, at the time a dirt road and a very sparsely populated area, from Miss Annie Heard who owned the Heard Estate. Appropriately, it had been used earlier for cattle grazing. Kay and Pete built a house on the lot, a rather average house for those times, with an eat-in kitchen, living room, dining room, three bedrooms, and a bath. Timothy Neil arrived on May 28, 1950, and the Turnham family settled into its new Auburn home and busy life. Pete was working hard as a dairy specialist and Kay had opened one of the state's first pre-schools, Happy House School. The couple continued to become more active in their community and in First Baptist Church, Pete as the director of the Sunday evening Training Union program. A few years after purchasing the lot for the house, Pete was able to buy more adjacent land expanding the property to six acres.

Pete planted a large vegetable garden in his back yard, which produced enough to keep his family fed and to give to friends. He said, "I was an avid gardener. I planted corn, beans, peas, tomatoes, okra, peppers, and many other things." And, Pete continued planting a garden each year until he was in his mid 90s. His daughter, Diane, added that Pete often added black-eyed peas, eggplant, cabbages, and in cooler weather, green onions, turnip greens (with a few mustard greens mixed in to make them less bitter), a little broccoli, radishes, and

a couple of hot peppers. "Okra was a staple and I can remember his half peck basket sitting on the kitchen counter full of the beautiful pods. Mother always fussed about Daddy's dirty feet in the kitchen, but she bragged on his vegetables when we were eating them, and I'm sure it pleased him. And, I still remember watching Mother can big jars of green beans." She said his fig trees still produce sweet tender figs, and, long ago, he had a couple of pear trees and a few scuppernong vines. Remembering how her mother made fig and pear preserves, Diane still picks figs from the trees each year and now makes her own preserves. "When I was young, Colonel Compton, from across the street, would work hard on the corn with Daddy. They would put mineral oil into the tassels of each of the ears as they were growing and it held down caterpillars. Such patience! It was so sad when deer would get into the corn some years. Daddy always delighted in having some corn ready for the Fourth of July." Another memory is of when she and Tim would go with Pete to get chicken manure for the garden from beside the chicken houses at Auburn University. He had an old hand-made small trailer and worked hard to fill it up while Diane and Tim played.

1953 brought both sadness and joy to Pete. He lost his mother to cancer at only 63 years of age on June 29th. Talking about her to his daughter, Diane, more than 60 years later he said, "My Mama was so sweet!" Then, on December 28, 1953, daughter, Ruthmary Kay, was born, a delayed Christmas gift to all the family. Needing a bigger salary, Pete said, "I was making $100 a week with Auburn University, and

PETE, DIANE, TIM AND RUTHMARY

Marshall and Bruce offered me $125 a week. In the mean time, I had gotten a part time job with Olin Hill who operated a clothing store here."

Mr. Hill, a legend in Auburn, started selling tailor made clothes when he arrived from Notasulga in January of 1928. Always ready to measure to fit, he kept a tape measure around his neck and he soon became known as "The Man with the Tape." Pete said if anyone caught Mr. Hill without his tape he would give him a dollar. Oth-

41

ers remember that if caught without his tape he would outfit the person who caught him with a free suit of clothes. In addition to the business community, Mr. Hill served the religious community in Auburn. A member of the First Baptist Church, as was Pete, he traveled around the world with the Billy Graham team of Youth For Christ International in 1958 and 1959, and was partly responsible for bringing Graham to Auburn in 1965 to speak at the University. The Graham Crusade stipulated that the audience in the stadium for his talk would be open to all and a luncheon to follow the talk would have at least 25 ministers present, both black and white. Mr. Hill helped set up both the talk and luncheon, and through his efforts, felt he was a part of the peaceful integration of Auburn University. In business for 60 years, Mr. Hill retired at the end of 1988.

Helping Pete get ready for his interview with Marshall and Bruce, Pete said, Mr. Hill "put a temporary hem in some suit pants so I could go to the interview with Marshall and Bruce. He loaned me some money, and he drove me to the interview in Nashville." Pete got the job as the South Alabama sales representative of Marshall and Bruce Company, primarily selling and delivering record books (obsolete now, thanks to computers) to courthouses, city halls, and similar places. In his new job, Pete said he always tried to get home for the night, though occasionally was too far away and had to stay in a rooming house, a hotel, or with friends. Getting home after the children were in bed asleep was especially hard, he said, because he could not tuck them in and tell them good-night. But, usually he could get home in time for dinner.

Continuing to expand his church and community activities, by 1956 Pete was a new member of the Lee County School Board, treasurer of Alpha Gamma Rho (professional agriculture fraternity), deputy district director of Lions International, and a member of the American Legion. A life long tither and church worker, he was serving his eighth year as Training Union Director, was the Enlistment Vice President of the Brotherhood, and was a member of both the Board of Deacons and the Missions Committee at his church. In addition, he was attending and earning credits in the U.S. Army Intelligence School as a Captain in the Army Reserves. Through these many activities, Pete became a sought after speaker.

Entering the Alabama House of Representatives

~☙☙☙

The Alabama Legislature was founded in 1818 as a territorial legislature for the Alabama Territory. Following the federal Alabama Enabling Act of 1819 and the successful passage of the first Alabama Constitution in the same year, the Alabama General Assembly became a fully-fledged state legislature upon the territory's admission as a state on December 14, 1819. After World War II, the state capital was a site of important Civil Rights Movement activities. On December 1, 1955, in Montgomery, Mrs. Rosa Parks rejected a bus driver's order to relinquish her seat in the "colored section" to a white passenger, after the whites-only section on a city bus was filled. This violated the Alabama segregation laws, resulting in her arrest for civil disobedience, and was followed by an NAACP backed boycott by African-Americans, 80% of the passengers of city buses. Lasting for over a year, it was the first major direct action campaign of the post-war civil rights movement. Rev. Dr. Martin Luther King, the new pastor at Dexter Avenue Baptist Church near the state capital in Montgomery, led the boycott. In November 1956, the federal Montgomery bus lawsuit, Browder v. Gayle, succeeded. Continuing to fight integration, the Alabama Legislature created the Alabama State Sovereignty Commission, using taxpayer dollars, to function as a state intelligence agency spying on Alabama residents suspected of sympathizing with the Civil Rights Movement. Following a federal constitutional amendment banning the use of poll taxes (a tax levied for the privilege of voting that often kept the poor, and particularly minorities, from voting, due to lack of funds) in federal elections, the Voting Rights Act of 1965 authorizing federal oversight and enforcement of fair registration and elections, and the 1966 US Supreme Court ruling that poll taxes at any level were unconstitutional, African Americans began to register and vote in numbers proportional to their population. They were again elected to the state legislature and to county and city offices for the first time since the late 19th century, following the Civil War. Although required by the state constitution to redistrict after each decennial census, the Alabama legislature had not done so from the turn of the century to 1960. As a result, representation in the legislature did not reflect the state's population and was biased toward rural interests. Under the principle of one man, one vote, the United States Supreme Court ruled in Reynolds v. Sims in 1964 that representation in both houses of any state legislature needed to be based on population with apportionment of seats redistricted as needed according to the decennial census. When the ruling was finally implemented in Alabama in 1972, it resulted in the districts with major industrial cities gaining more seats in the legislature. It was during this tumultuous time in the history of Alabama that Pete entered, learned about, and established his place in Alabama politics.

The Alabama House of Representatives is the lower house of the Alabama General Assembly. Residents elect representatives from their geographic districts to represent them at the state level. Along with the counterparts in the state Senate, the upper house of the General Assembly, Representatives craft bills that address the needs of their communities and vote on their adoption to the state constitution. Representatives, like Senators, serve on committees that are responsible for vetting specific types of legislation and aid fellow lawmakers in focusing on specific issues. As in the federal government, the Alabama House of Representatives is responsible for controlling state spending allocations. Whereas both Representatives and Senators can craft bills, only Representatives can introduce spending bills that fund state agencies, operations, and other projects. Along with only four other states, Alabama Representatives are elected for four- year terms. At the beginning of each term, or quadrennium, the House holds an organizational session during which officers are elected, procedural rules are adopted, committee members are appointed, and any restructuring takes place. Legislative business is conducted in a part-time session from January to April. Sessions last no more than 30 legislative days within a 105-day calendar period, unless the governor calls a special session to complete important business.

In November of 1958 Pete won his first election, as a Democrat, to represent Lee County, and, immediately following the election, was sworn in as a member of the Alabama House of Representatives, his term to begin in January 1958. He said he was part of a group in Lee County that was looking for a young candidate to run for a seat in the state legislature. When the group met to share their views on whom that candidate should be, he got some unexpected news. "We all met, and everybody asked each other 'Have you decided who you want?' And, I said, 'Well, I've been gone all week, and I really haven't.' 'Well,' they said, 'That's all right. We have.' I said 'Who did you all pick?' They said, 'You.' I said, 'I'll tell you what I'll do. I'll serve one term, four years, and then I'm coming home.' They said, 'Okay.' So I took it, got elected, and stayed there forty years. I said, 'That's just like a politician, saying you're going to stay four years, and you stay forty!' " Upon winning his first election, Pete published a thank you to the constituents in District 79 saying:

1959 - PETE AND KAY AT THEIR FIRST GOVERNOR'S INAUGURAL BALL

It is with deep gratitude and humility that I offer my sincere thanks to the voters of Lee County for your wonderful support in Tuesday's election.

I repeat my pledge to give you the very best representation in the State Legislature – in agriculture, education, and industry. I will exert every effort to improve the lot of our farmers, achieve more adequate financial support for our public schools and colleges, and attract new industry for our fine county.

I shall always be ready to discuss our county and state problems with you and will welcome your suggestions and comments. Working together, we can insure Lee County's position at the top of the list.

Sincerely,
Pete Turnham

As a new member of the House of Representatives, Pete said, "I took a lot of hard licks learning, and some of the old seasoned members took advantage of the new members. I learned gradually by losing some battles and winning some." As a more seasoned member, he learned how the system worked and how to get bills introduced and passed. "When you strike up a bill, like the kindergarten bill", said

Pete, "it becomes very popular, and the people back home realize the Senator and Representative are sincere and passionate, and you become name-worthy after that. It's more or less trial and error, hard work, and hard licks." Pete had friends in the House he thought a lot of and those friends thought a lot of Pete. "I had friends who came and sat with me and explained a bill, and would say, 'Here is why this is needed.' Then I'd join up with them and pass it. Then others would say, 'Man, how'd ya'll pass that bill?' and we'd say, 'We just got on the mic and sold it!'" Pete says it's a hard job passing legislation because a bill is introduced, goes to committee, is debated in committee, and, if it passes, one has to work to get it on top of the calendar. Finally, it must be put on special order and gotten through committee. He added, "Some of that stuff in Washington takes years!" When asked if it ever took him more than a year to get something passed he answered yes. "You try to elect a speaker who will be fair to you and sometimes it's hard to get that done." Overall, he said he was pretty lucky, about average on most of it, because he didn't have much controversial legislation. Learning quickly, by 1959 Pete was on the State Administration, Education, and Local Government committees. He co-sponsored four bills which became law – (1) raising the compensation of the deputies to the sheriff of Lee County, (2) raising the compensation of the county solicitor, (3) providing for the re-identification of electors (purging and updating the voter lists) in Lee County, and (4) amending the act which created and established the Court of Common Pleas of Lee County, restructuring the court and establishing compensation for the new positions. In April of that year, while addressing the Ozark Kiwanis Club, he told the members that education topped the list of problems that must be solved in the next session of the legislature. "We train teachers in seven state supported institutions and lose them to other states every year, which is poor economy for us to be practicing," he said, an early indication education would be the primary focus of his 40 years in the legislature.

Effective September 21, 1959, by direction of the President, Pete was promoted to the rank of Major in the Army Reserve. A firm believer in the oft quoted point that "a well informed America is our first line of defense," Pete stated that a major reason for his membership in the active Reserve lay in the fact that his Reserve service provided up-to-the-minute information required to keep his people abreast of advancements in the system of national defense.

With great anticipation and completing the Turnham family, son Joseph Rice was born on October 28, 1959. Needing more room in the family home, an addition was added to the rear on one side; two bedrooms, one for Diane and one for Tim. A few

PETE AND KAY WITH TIM,
RUTHMARY, AND JOE

years later an expanded kitchen, a den, an office, and a bath, with a carport underneath, were added. When all the children were grown and had left home, Pete and Kay turned the back two bedrooms into a master bedroom with a master bath.

In July of 1960, Pete went before the House Ways and Means Committee to request approval of a bill upping the corporate income tax from 3 to 5 percent, providing an additional $5.5 million a year for schools. The current state school superintendent, Bing LeCroy, said Alabama was investing less money per school child than any of the 49 other states. Pete said if nothing was done for the schools, "You will see schools close. . . you will see teachers leave in great numbers" during the coming year."

Notes from speeches Pete made through the years tell much about who he is. His passion was and is education, and the following are notes he made for a speech in 1960.

1. *Prone to look at 1959…*

2. *Auburn and Lee County came out okay on bond issue*

3. *In education, we must always look ahead. Progress never stands still*

4. *We can never build a great state on ignorance and skimping on educational expenditures.*

5. *Education cuts across the entire economy of our state.*

    a. Public schools

    b. Universities and Colleges

    c. Trade schools

    d. Vocational Agriculture

    e. Extension Service

    f. Private Schools

6. *1960 - we spent $135.3 Million*

    1961 - we expect 137.9 Million

    1962 - we expect 148.0 Million

> 7. *We need at this moment: 16 million to hold our own and 25 million to get ahead.*

As Pete began his tenure in the legislature, Kay was working on her degree at Auburn in Family Life and Early Childhood Education in the School of Home Economics. They had recently helped establish a mission church, Lakeview Baptist, and Kay helped organize and became the superintendent of the Beginner Department. Early in their marriage, Kay had felt called to go into the teaching field after she began teaching Sunday School in the Auburn First Baptist Church, and she felt she needed to get her degree in education to be able to become fully effective in the field. Taking a full load of courses for a year, while teaching three hours each day in the university kindergarten and managing her busy household of four children, Kay received her degree in March 1961.

MARCH 1961 - KAY RECEIVES HER FIRST MASTER'S DEGREE

SUPPORT
PETE TURNHAM
FOR RE-ELECTION
STATE REPRESENTATIVE
LEE COUNTY
For Honest, Clean Government
SUBJECT TO ACTION SPEC. DEMOCRATIC PRIMARY, AUG. 28, 1962
Pd. Pol. Adv. by Pete Turnham, Auburn, Ala.

By 1961, Pete had become involved with the Alabama Mental Health Association, serving on the Board of Directors of that organization. Mental health became another strong interest during his tenure in the legislature, along with education and local government. He was elected that same year for a second four-year term in the House of Representatives.

In 1962 Pete was elected Chairman of the House Education Committee, a position he would maintain for seventeen years, and was appointed a member of the Ways and Means Committee. He was the author of the school amendment allowing counties to raise the constitutional tax limit from 7 to 12 mils. Pete also completed the National Security Seminar conducted by the Industrial College of the Armed Forces, and was asked to be the alumnus speaker at the Special Orientation Course at the Army's Command and General Staff College at Ft. Leavenworth, Kansas, that summer. His topic was "The Role of the Civilian in the Army Information Program".

In February 1963, the Russell County Mental Health Association was organized, and unanimously adopted a plan to operate a proposed East Alabama Mental Health Clinic to be located in Opelika and to serve six counties; Lee, Russell, Bullock, Bar-

1962 - THE PETE TURNHAM FAMILY

bour, Macon, and Tallapoosa. In a principal address to the association on April 29, Pete said the state's interim committee on mental health was receiving strong opposition to a plan to take the mental hygiene division out from under the control of the State Health Department and establish it as a separate administrative department of the state. He said Alabama had only two psychiatrists for about 10,000 inmates and ranked 42nd in its per capita contribution to mental health work.

"Public sentiment can be pretty cruel at times," he said. "For each letter of support we receive in the legislature, we get 10 to 15 in opposition. Mental health is the most challenging phase of our government today, and we had better accept the challenge, and do something about the problem."

His notes for that meeting were:

A talk to the Russell County Mental Health Association on April 29, 1963…

Open with prayer…

Tell a few jokes…

    I. 1 out of 10 suffer from mental illness enough for treatment

    II. 18 million Americans suffer – six times the population of Alabama

    III. We spend 4 billion dollars a year on it - 1 out of 2 beds is occupied by a mental patient

    IV. 50% of 22 million patients admitted last year were from mental troubles

    V. Increase in juvenile delinquency, crime, suicide, divorce, drug addiction, traffic accidents, and chronic alcoholism - These were largely rooted in mental emotions.

    VI. The future looks good – Average per diem appropriation for all state hospitals is $5.00 per day –

        1. Alabama, $3.00 as of last year

        2. Alabama Association of Mental Health is asking for $1.00 increase this year

3. *Expansion of mental health clinics*

4. *$3 million bond issue*

5. *Follow up and small centers –*

VII. *Mental Health Study Committee by House and Senate of 1961 – Recommended – State Department of Mental Health*

   1. *17 member board represented by:*

      1. *Doctors, 2. Laymen, 3. Psychologists, 4. Others*

   2. *This board takes the case to the people -*

   3. *Alabama needs to look at herself and what she is doing -*

   4. *Situation at Bryce and Searcy hospitals and Partlow State Schools – Bad*

   5. *Boards have never appeared and asked us for help -*

   6. *Future legislation – The following facts are supplied by the Regional Office of the United States Public Health Service in Atlanta: Per Capita Income (1961) and State Per Capita Appropriations for Public Health in 1962:*

Alabama-	*$1,492*	*$3.61*
Mississippi-	*$1,229*	*$ .95*
South Carolina -	*$1,433*	*$1.07*

   Per Capita Expenditures for Community Mental Health Program:

U. S. Averages	*$.36*	*Rank*
Alabama	*.10*	*42*
Georgia	*.23*	*23*
South Carolina	*.12*	*39*

The task is challenging. The opportunity is upon us.
Our efforts must point toward an early solution.
Your organization can help! Annual meeting in Montgomery – June 4th – Joint session with speaker

In September, he addressed the District III Alabama Education Association Annual meeting; and, as the legislature ended its 1963 session that month, Pete was voted one of the three hardest working representatives by the biennial poll of capital newsmen. As the current president of the Lee County Health Center Board, in October he was elected president of the Alabama Rehabilitation Association where Dr. Frank Echols, supervisor of rehabilitation services in Florida, addressed the group and said, "We can't rehabilitate disabilities, we must rehabilitate persons. We can't have a happy community if many people are in a state of dependency." He challenged the group to be concerned about the groups they were not rehabilitating so well, emphasizing mentally handicapped and recovered mentally ill patients, a challenge Pete accepted and fought hard for during his years in the legislature.

Addressing school transportation leaders in March 1964, Pete told them Alabama could develop its total economic picture through raising its educational standing. Mentioning some industries which had taken a look at Alabama and moved on to settle in other states, Pete said those businesses were not concerned about the state's tax structure but the fact that the schools were not up to where it was thought they should be. Emphasizing the state needed to contribute more to education he said, "If we are going to save our democracy it must start at the local level. The sooner we can become less dependent upon the next echelon of government, the better off we will be."

On June 6, 1964, Pete made a speech to the Columbus, Georgia, Credit Bureau using the following notes:

Open with prayer -

Free Enterprise

1. *Our system of Government*
   Legislative
   Executive
   Judicial
2. *Great Struggle in every state and in Washington is for one to take over the other -*
3. *Our system, though not perfect, is the best yet. I'll take it until something better comes along -*
4. *Our government, whether intentional or not, has a tendency to gradually take over and regulate free enterprise in America –*
5. *One basis of free enterprise is complete freedom to experiment, venture,*

develop, and *produce*, *without interference or restraint, except for certain safeguards, which protect the rights of others – Another basis of free enterprise is to enjoy the fruits of* <u>one's own labor.</u>

6. *Free enterprise was born in Jamestown, Va., after an attempt at socialism almost ended in disaster for the community because there was stronger desire for equal share than to contribute equal work. This is the fundamental error of socialism –*

Our pilgrim fathers had the same experience. They first agreed that everything would be owned in common, but they lost their initiative and nearly starved to death-

During the Revolutionary War the Continental Congress took over the economic controls of the 13 colonies, but they met disaster by such poor results and our forefathers, freed from restraint, went on to win their freedom-

190 years ago men of experience gave the world a new nation, conceived in liberty, and they prayed that future generations would remain free forever.

<u>Washington said</u>: *"Government is not reason, it is not eloquence… it is a force! Like fire, it is a dangerous servant and a fearful master."*

<u>Madison said</u>: *"I believe there are more instances of the abridgement of the freedom of the people by gradual and silent encroachment of those in power than by violent and sudden usurpations."*

None of our early presidents ever proposed any legislation that would interfere with or regulate private control of industry and agriculture.

Under the philosophy of free enterprise, which was followed uniformly by every president until 1932, America plunged ahead.

By 1900 we had shown the rest of the world a true example of free enterprise. There was more steel produced in Pittsburgh than in all of England and Germany combined. Americans then had the highest standard of living of any country in the world.

With the coming of the depression in the '30's, we began to lose faith in our own integrity and resourcefulness and to rely on the paternalism of government. Up until then, uniform decisions of the Supreme Court had consistently followed the philosophy of our founding fathers. Those decisions prevented the government from unduly regulating the lives of the people. But in the 30's new justices were appointed to the Supreme Court, who for better or for worse, did not confine their duties to interpreting the Constitution in the light of its history and language, but imported social concepts which were foreign to our basic philosophy. With this change Congress then became the last stronghold for the defense of freedom against government intervention. But instead of holding the line, Congress seized the opportunity to curtail free enterprise and enlarge government. This is a serious charge. Let me try to prove it.

1. *In 1920, government owned public utilities accounted for 5% of the electric power generated. Today 25%.*

2. *One out of every six employed Americans is now on a national, state or local payroll. 17 million people receive checks from the Federal government, 143,000 in Alabama alone are on welfare.*

3. *Federal aid to states, local governments, and individuals was less than $150 million in 1930. Today this aid totals over $10 billion dollars.*

4. *In 1932, before President Roosevelt came to power, the governmenttent collected $2,634,000,000 in revenues. In 1964 it collected $93,000,000,000, an increase of 100% for each of the intervening years.*

5. *In 1932 the federal debt was $22.5 billion dollars. Today it is more than $300 billion dollars.*

Jefferson said: "A wise and frugal government can restrain men singly or in groups from injuring one another without telling them what to sow and when and how to reap it.

A wise and frugal government would punish crime but it would otherwise leave men free to govern themselves according to the Ten Commandments of God, rather than undertake to force universal compliance with tens of thousands of commands of government.

A wise and frugal government would not engage in 19,000 different businesses or own 21 percent of the land in America.

A wise and frugal government does not, except in times of great emergency and national peril, pay for its debts out of money which remains in the pockets of its citizens after they have paid their taxes."

This simply is not AMERICANISM!

<u>*Remedies to bring our country back to its "normal" health....*</u>

1. *First, we must rededicate ourselves to the cause of freedom and free enterprise. To believe in it we must practice it. We cannot live by a double standard of criticizing the government for giving handouts to certain groups and then eating out of the public trough ourselves. If we are critical of the Federal government using our taxes for slum clearance in New York City, we have no right to ask the government to build federal power plants for our cities and states in the south.*

2. *Be willing to finance those who fight our battles to preserve free enterprise.*

3. *Back the philosophy of giving to our country, rather than taking from it. This is true Americanism.*

4. *Teach the gospel of free enterprise in our schools. Three-fourths of the states do not require courses in economics in high school (1 out of 20).*

5. *Government must observe the Golden Rule of doing for one group what it does for another.*

6. *Sixth and last, we must constantly remind ourselves that we are a Republic and not a Democracy in the truest sense. As provided in the Constitution of the Nation or the State, we periodically elect representatives who, having been installed in office, may vote as they please and according to their own consciences. If the Republic is to survive we must first make sure that the candidate for whom we shall vote is honest, trustworthy, and will not only support the Constitution, but will only introduce and vote for legislation which will protect private enterprise against excessive*

controls by Big Government. We must make certain that
our candidate believes in the philosophy that government is derived
only from the consent of the governed. Know our politicians
and express our views!

Early in 1964 Pete decided to run for Judge of Probate in Lee County. It was the one position he ran for and did not get. Ted Little, a friend who was elected to the State Senate in 1974, said it was because Pete's constituency knew they had the best man in the best position where he was in the legislature, and they did not want to change it.

In early 1965 Pete was appointed by Governor Wallace as the Alabama representative to the Southern Interstate Nuclear Board, an assignment that would begin forty-five years of dedicated service and leadership.

The Southern States Energy Board

On August 6, 1945, during World War II, at 8:16 AM, an American B-29 bomber dropped the world's first deployed atomic bomb over the Japanese city of Hiroshima, Japan. The power of the blast was the equivalent of destruction resulting from 12,000 to 15,000 tons of TNT. Approximately 80,000 people were killed and another 35,000 were injured, followed by another 60,000 who would be dead by the end of the year from the effects of the fallout. Three days later another bomb was dropped on Nagasaki, killing an estimated 40,000 people, and effectively ending the war.

Even before the war, a group of American scientists had become concerned with nuclear weapons research being conducted in Nazi Germany. As a result, in 1940, the U.S. government began funding its own atomic weapons development program which came, after the U.S. entry into the war, under the joint responsibility of the Office of Scientific Research and Development and the War Department. Over the next few years the program's scientists worked on producing the key materials for nuclear fission-uranium-235 and plutonium, and on July 16, 1945, the first successful test of the bomb, called the Manhattan Project, was conducted. America had entered the atomic age.

The use of the atomic bomb proved its destructive power, but there were those who believed the power could and should be used for the good of mankind. A special congressional panel, the Senate-House Joint Committee on Atomic Energy, soon concluded that control of such force should be transferred from military to civilian authority. As a result, the Atomic Energy Act of 1946, signed by President Harry

Truman, created a five-man board, named the Atomic Energy Commission, to guide future research and applications while safeguarding present control and utilization.

The Tennessee Valley Authority (TVA), established in 1933 as part of President Franklin Roosevelt's "New Deal" to bring energy resources to un-served and poorly served households, businesses, and industries in the south, helped to establish the south as a driving force in the effort to find ways to use nuclear power for the good of mankind. In 1943 the construction of the Oak Ridge National Laboratory in Oak Ridge, Tennessee, was tasked with the production of the uranium isotope U-235 to serve as atomic bomb fuel. Later, under the control of the Atomic Energy Commission, the Oak Ridge Lab insured the south had a major role in the development of nuclear power in the future.

After the Soviet Union exploded an atomic bomb in 1949, President Truman pressed the Atomic Energy Commission to pursue research on all varieties of atomic weapons, particularly the hydrogen, or super, bomb. A 200,000 acre tract in the south near Aiken, South Carolina, with close proximity to Augusta, Georgia, was chosen as the site of the facility to be built to produce the materials for the bombs. This facility would be known as the Savannah River Plant. Four years after its construction, in 1954, the first shipment of plutonium left its gates. In the 1950s, in an effort to find a key element, uranium, for atomic/nuclear fuel, a massive phosphate-rich region centered east of Tampa, Florida was discovered, again bringing the south into the forefront of nuclear development.

At the end of his first year as president, on December 8, 1953, former World War II hero Dwight Eisenhower spoke before the General Assembly of the United Nations and called for an International Atomic Energy Agency for the furtherance of "the peaceful pursuits of mankind". He pledged that the United States would help "find the way by which the miraculous inventiveness of man shall not be dedicated to his death, but consecrated to his life." By mid 1954 he approved amendments to the Atomic Energy Act of 1946, which permitted private concerns to harness the potential of nuclear energy for power.

LeRoy Collins was elected governor of Florida in January 1955, and he became a driving force for the peaceful use of nuclear power, first for his state and later for the south. That September he arrived in Point Clear, Alabama for his first Southern Governors' Conference, where he advocated that the south should grow with the atom, "making industry follow the atom and not stand idly by and permit the atom to follow existing industry." From his advocacy the "Point Clear Plan" was established, whereby Southern states would coordinate the possible development of civilian uses of nuclear energy in the region. With success at the conference promoting his ideas, he convened the following January a preliminary conference at Oak Ridge, Tennessee, "to promote nuclear industrial development on a region-wide basis." In attendance were fifty-two "technical and educational experts from sixteen Southern and border states" and "fifteen special consultants familiar with nuclear energy developments throughout the country." He envisioned the south providing leadership in the future to developments that would help all humanity. Under the auspices of the Southern Regional Education Board, Governor Collins convened a "Work Conference on Nuclear Energy" at Redington Beach, Florida, on August 1, 1956, which urged Southern governors to create "statewide atomic energy citizens advisory committees." The result was the creation of a Regional Advisory Council on Nuclear Energy for the purpose of fully exploring the advisability of the establishment of a compact, participated in by the states represented at the conference for development of nuclear energy, for the advancement of the region. That organization convened in Atlanta in February 1957, with fourteen states in attendance. The work done at that conference and continued work by the Regional Advisory Council on Nuclear Energy culminated in the establishment, at the Southern Governors' Conference in October 1959, of the Southern Interstate Nuclear Compact. The compact called for a regional board to be composed of one member from each state, who, in most cases, was appointed by the governor. It also provided for a nonvoting federal representative to be appointed by the President of the United States, a first for an interstate compact agency. The powers of the compact were (1) to encourage the development and use of nuclear energy, facilities, installations, and products, (2) to gather and disseminate information on the nonmilitary uses of nuclear energy, (3) to conduct or assist in training programs for state and local personnel in the field and provide aid in formulating and administering safety measures, and (4) to recommend changes in state laws and regulations to achieve uniformity where possible. Ratification by each state was finally completed in June 1961, and the Southern Interstate Nuclear Board was empowered by the state governors on September 27, 1961, to organize and begin operations with eight states participating. The remaining states of the original compact continued to pass legislation until the last one signed in 1966. Meanwhile, Congress gave its consent to the Southern Interstate Nuclear Compact and authorized a federal representative for the board. Passing through the House and the Senate, President John F. Kennedy signed the Southern Interstate Nuclear Compact into law on July 31, 1962. From its Atlanta headquarters, the Southern Interstate Nuclear

Board leadership set its course, moving nuclear technology from the laboratory to the marketplace. With major changes, from leadership to acceptance of a broader area of responsibility, the governors of the southern region renamed the Southern Interstate Nuclear Board in 1977 as the Southern States Energy Board.

Serving at the time as a Major in the Military Intelligence Service in the Army Reserves, Pete Benton Turnham was appointed in 1965 by Alabama Governor George Wallace as the Alabama representative to the Southern Interstate Nuclear Board. Within three years members recognized his leadership abilities and elected him treasurer in 1968 and chairman in 1975.

1968 - SINB EXECUTIVE COMMITTEE MEMBERS
SEATED LEFT TO RIGHT - ROBERT H. GIFFORD, PETE B. TURNHAM, DR. JOHN J. MCKETTER
STANDING LEFT TO RIGHT - ROBERT C. BLAIR, DONALD J. WHITTINGHILL, VICTOR S. JOHNSON, AND DR. DANIEL S. APPLEBAUM

In April 1972, another driving force, Kenneth Nemeth, joined the Southern Interstate Nuclear Board as assistant to the executive director in the position of director of intergovernmental programs and became SINB Secretary and Executive Director in February 1975. Ken, a graduate of Florida State University in Government (now Political Science), had served, while a student, as governor of the Florida district of Circle K International, the collegiate Kiwanis organization. He also served a year as commissioner of elections and another year as secretary of state for student government. Some of his particular fields of interest were agriculture and rural development, energy, environment, and solid waste. After graduation he began law school at FSU while working for the Speaker of the Florida House of Representatives, Richard Pettigrew, who wanted to develop legislation that would reorganize state government in Florida. As a member of the group of young law students working for Speaker Pettigrew, Ken helped get the legislation passed. Soon after the legislation was passed he received a call from a friend in Atlanta who said the Council of State Governments in Atlanta was looking for someone to come in and be a governmental reorganization specialist because there were several states wanting to do what Florida had done. Ken took the job and made the move to Atlanta. The Council of State Governments staffed the Southern States Governors Conference. Through this organization Ken met the aides to the governors, and James T. Goodwin was one of those aides. Jim served as the Texas coordinator of natural resources and environmental advisor to Governor Preston Smith; and, in January 1972, had accepted the position of Executive Director of the Southern Interstate Nuclear Board. In March, he called Ken and said he needed someone who understood the legislatures, because the legislatures provided all the funding for the SINB. Ken knew those people, and he began work for the Southern Interstate Nuclear Board on April 15th.

With so many interests in common, politics, Kiwanis Club (Pete was an active member in Auburn), and agriculture and rural development, it seemed inevitable Pete and Ken would form a bond quickly. Ken said, "Pete was my mentor. He was the person who took me under his wing. When I joined the organization, my first job on my first day was to get on a plane in Atlanta and fly to Austin, Texas for the Southern Interstate Nuclear Board's 12th annual meeting. At that meeting in Austin I met Pete Turnham. We talked. We got along really well. We sat together. We hit it off. The next day, August 15, our board members had a lunch of 'kilowatt catfish', which were grown in the nuclear effluent outside a nuclear power plant, to show us that catfish could be grown safely in the warm water. After lunch we boarded a bus and drove for five hours to Rock Springs, Texas, to a large preserve where they had all kinds of animals from Africa and around the world. It was a retreat for the board to discuss what programs they were doing, what they wanted to pursue, and how they wanted to move forward."

Just two years later, Jim Goodwin developed lung cancer and stepped down as the SINB executive director. After an extensive search for his replacement, which included over 400 applicants, the Board chose Ken Nemeth to lead the organization in February of 1975.

Later in 1975, just after Pete was elected chairman, the Honorable Pedro G. Zorilla Martinez, governor of the Mexican State of Nuevo Leon, was present at the board meeting and requested his designation as an associate

PETE AND KEN NEMETH PREPARE THE CHAIRMAN'S MESSAGE TO THE BOARD AT SOUTHERN STATES NUCLEAR BOARD 1975 ANNUAL MEETING

PETE AND GOVERNOR PEDRO G. ZORILLA MARTINEZ OF THE MEXICAN STATE OF NUEVO LEON SPEAKING AT A MEETING IN MONTEREY

member. The board explored the request and extended an invitation. A delegation, including Pete and Ken, visited Monterey and talked about oil and gas production, new priorities, nuclear safety, nuclear fuel cycles, education, needs for energy technology, etc. Per Ken, "It was a great opportunity to connect with a country which is a part of North America and which was very interested in selling natural gas to the United States. Our meetings were the initial move in that direction."

Soon after joining SINB, Ken initiated a variety of measures to improve public relations and information dissemination capabilities, one a newsletter intended for regional dissemination called SINB State Action Report. As the newsletters circulated and publications mounted, so, too, did the board's commitment to serve as a vital information resource. Under Chairman Turnham, it pursued development of a regional energy information system keyed to a resource library at SINB headquarters. "We need it, "Pete explained, "because the states have a great deal at stake here. I want this capability so that state governments and all of our educational institutions can get credible information on science and technology." SINB had changed from a promotional board for nuclear energy to a trusted, non-partisan advisory body on all energy matters.

On May 23, 1976, Pete's second year as chairman, he opened the board meeting in Winston-Salem, North Carolina, with these words: *"Honored speakers, members of SINB, and distinguished guests.... It is my privilege and pleasure to appear before you as the 1975-76 chairman of SINB and call this 15th annual meeting to order. This has truly been an outstanding year for the board. It has been marked by the great dedication of our members and a super effort by the SINB staff. I think that this will be evident to you as you listen to our guest speakers and hear of our accomplishments. As SINB chairman, I have traveled through our member states and made many new friends. Sometimes I was amazed by how many interests our states have in common. Although the southern region is diverse in its utilization of fuels and energy... we have states which depend primarily on coal, oil, gas, and nuclear power.... all areas of the region are experiencing serious energy problems. Even Puerto Rico, which is one of our distinguished member jurisdictions, finds itself almost totally dependent on the whims of the petroleum market. My point is this.... The energy problems which we now face will become more severe unless the states become increasingly aggressive toward the development of a comprehensive energy policy. As the energy arm of the southern governors, SINB will be heavily involved in the formulation of these critical policies during the coming year. We will solicit the support and input of state decision-makers throughout the region in order to give us a firmer foundation on which to build our programs.".....*

Perhaps more than any other board officer, Pete would influence the Southern Interstate Nuclear Board and its successor, the Southern States Energy Board, in the decades immediately following his elevation to the chairmanship in 1975. Ken said, "Pete's mentorship of me evolved when he became chairman, matured in the position, and as he began to see the direction in which he thought the board needed to go. He strongly believed that while nuclear issues were very important, as well as space, science, and technology issues, because of the diversity in the southern region in having states that have coal, states that have oil, states that have gas, that we should look into expanding the board's purview into all of those areas, so that it would be an energy board versus a nuclear board. Those were discussions Pete had substantively with the governors at the time and with the members of the board, to the point where they could see the utility in us having a change in our name and, also, some changes in the compact of broadening to all forms of energy. And, they wanted environmental issues under the Board's purview, too, because they felt like that was a critical piece of any energy program."

By the mid 70s the nation had begun to forget about the energy crisis of 1973-74 and, as a result, the nation's leadership was backing away from addressing all the challenges of the era. That indifference created the opportunity, in Pete's vision, for the SINB to fill a critical need. At a time when greater questions of energy supply and demand, coupled with environmental impact, were being ignored, his organization would emphasize knowledge and the need for action. It would do so across the broad spectrum of the energy and environmental topic. "It's difficult enough to understand many of the major problems of our day," Pete said. "The people must know what our major energy options are so that choices can be made. We're going to run out of oil and gas in the next several decades if we're not careful. Coal and nuclear power are obvious answers, but they have drawbacks. A balanced economy needs a corresponding effort in energy development with respect for our environment. We must provide opportunities for the people to speak." This was the beginning of the Southern Interstate Nuclear Board becoming the Southern States Energy Board.

By 1977, at the beginning of Jimmy Carter's presidency, President Carter called for a direct assault on energy dependence. His plan incorporated specific goals to be reached by 1985, and congress acted within four months to prepare the federal government for implementation of the new national energy policy. When the newly formed Department of Energy began operations on October 1, 1977, the Southern Interstate Nuclear Board had been involved for months in helping to plan development and implementation of the still-to-be-finalized national energy program.

When the Southern Governors' Conference voted in August of 1977 to rename the SINB as the Southern States Energy Board, Chairman Turnham created two task forces to facilitate the reorganization, and on December 19, 1977, the executive committee met in Atlanta and unanimously approved the move to begin using the name Southern States Energy Board no later than February 15, 1978. With the name change came concerns by the Southern Governors' Conference about the makeup of the board, particularly as more federal funds were being acquired. According to Ken, "Pete was the leader of the whole idea to expand the board. He had meetings with members of the legislative council and

KAY AND PETE IN CENTER - AT THE 1978 ANNUAL MEETING OF THE SSEB

64

council directors around the region to talk about it. He helped put together the language that made the changes in the board so that we would become the Southern States Energy Board. In 1978-79, the states all passed legislation superseding the Southern Interstate Nuclear Compact and the Southern Interstate Nuclear Board to become the Southern States Energy Compact and the Southern States Energy Board. Pete played a major role in that, and we would probably not be here today if it wasn't for those activities, because that really got us out there." Led by Chairman Turnham, the new SSEB compact included governors and state legislators as members.

There were both oil and gas in many southern states and the new thing called nuclear, which the southern states were evolving and absorbing, resulting in more and more nuclear plants being built in the region. Today the south has almost 50% of the nuclear power in the country, plus the federal repositories and federal laboratories, like Oakridge National Lab and Savannah River National Laboratory. Per Ken, "Not only did we have the plants themselves, we had the technology and all the aspects of the fuel cycle. We went from the preparation of uranium to be used in a nuclear power plant all the way through to where the real secretive stuff began, when they began putting tritium in the nuclear bombs. We were also using radioisotopes in various medical procedures, like medical identification of tumors. We were laminating doors with radioactive materials and making wood plastics out of them so they wouldn't burn."

"President Franklin Roosevelt had many programs in the south, like the Tennessee Valley Authority, to bring electricity, indoor plumbing, etc., to the region, which other parts of the country already had. The governors wanted to change the perception of the south as being backward; and, with all the natural energy resources in the south, the opportunity was there to move to the forefront with nuclear power. Along with this effort was public education and outreach, expanding universities to build the work force to manage various programs, and to build, through technology development, a competent workforce that would know how to work on nuclear power plants, how to run a nuclear power plant, and actually build the plants."

Pete continued to come back to the fact that SSEB was an interstate organization and states had to work together for the common good. From that, a database was built, one which is still used today. Ken said, "We can print out one piece of paper on each state which will show our projects, the different programs, the meetings held there, and the cost of those meetings (because that is economic development), plus any specific requests made by the governor, the state legislature, or by industry. We also include any consultants who work for us in the state. I'm proud to say that today, in the south, we fund 31 state universities. I think the basic principle which Pete championed, was to perform essential services for state governments that they can't do for themselves. There are so many issues and problems that always have been regional in nature. An example is an air quality zone, which stretches through several states. It doesn't cut off at the border between states. There are rivers that form state borders, which are interstate issues. And, there are lots of areas where states can learn from each other. One of the ways to do that is to have meetings on topics which are of great interest to the states, or that will enable, for example, a legislator from one state to listen to a presentation from a legislator in another state, feel it is needed in his or her own state, then take that legislation and introduce it in his state. We also began to understand that if we could manage projects that may not help all our 16 states and 2 territories, but would help the region, either by developing technologies, or by managing a group of experts who would help the region, who

KEN NEMETH

would develop better energy technology, pollute less, use less fuel, and enable power plants to run longer periods of time between their maintenance periods, it would build up, not only the value of that energy, but our ability to say to all the companies which have come into the south, 'We have the energy and power to enable you to build your manufacturing facilities.' "

One time, during Pete's tenure as chairman, he and Ken were flying to Charleston, West Virginia. They had a 6:30 AM flight and, according to Ken, "It was in mid January and it was snowing. When we landed at the Charleston airport we skidded off the runway. When we did, I grabbed Pete's hand and Pete grabbed my hand, and we just sat there. We looked around and, sure enough, airport personnel came out with all the emergency equipment. It was a tough one." Finally able to leave, they rented a car, went to the state legislature, and spent all day. "We walked into offices, and, with Pete with me, it was transformational, because, when a legislator sees one of their own, it's a peer to peer meeting. He told stories and put everybody at ease. We were having a problem with the appropriations from the state, and they were asking what we had done for them lately. We knew what we had done, we knew we had worked with their people, their universities, and other organizations. We were so small, six people on our staff, and how did people find out about us? Pete! It was an amazing thing. " Continuing his description of Pete, Ken said, "I would pick up the

Turnham family, and she would often work on those football weekend Saturdays to help with preparations.

A fond family memory retold often was of the time, after everyone had left, when Kay asked Pete, "Who was that young couple who parked on the side of the road in front of the house?" She described them and Pete remembered them but said, "I don't know." They chuckled and said they guessed the people saw the party and decided to stop by for free food.

In later years, Pete's company bought scholarship seats so Pete, Kay, and guests would have a reserved parking space and covered seats. It enabled them to continue to attend games as well as support the Auburn scholarship program.

Continuing to Move Forward and Take On More Responsibility

In addition to his new responsibilities with the Southern States Energy Board in 1965, Pete was also a member of the Southern Regional Committee on Agriculture and a member of the Alabama Legislative Study Committee on Higher Education. Always seeking to improve education, he introduced a bill to raise the salary of the state superintendent of education, something that had not been done in several years. The salary at that time was $10,000, far below what many other educational officials in the state were making, and the salary was raised to $18,000, effective when the next superintendent took office.

Perhaps Pete's proudest accomplishment was sponsorship of the largest bond issue for school buildings in the history of Alabama, a $116 million bond issue passed in the 1965 special legislative session, providing for new and updated schools all over the state. Pete received a letter in May from Dr. E. V. Smith, Dean and Director of the School of Agriculture and Agricultural Experiment Station System at Auburn University.

May 10, 1965

Dear Pete,

As you know, I had no direct contact with the legislature during its recent successful session. Nevertheless, I had both a personal and a profession-

73

al interest in its proceedings. Consequently, I followed the reports in the news media and the reports that Dr. Anderson made on occasion to the Administrative Council with great interest. As the Dean and Director of the School of Agriculture and as a member of the Alpha Gamma Rho fraternity, I have taken great pride in the prominent role that our alumnus, Pete B. Turnham, has played in all legislation for education. I also congratulate you on your appointment to membership on the Southern Nuclear Board. I know that you will provide aggressive leadership there.

Yours very truly,
E. V. Smith

When long time Auburn University president Ralph B. Draughon retired in 1965, the new president, Harry M. Philpott, wrote the following letter to Pete on May 25th.

Dear Mr. Turnham,

Thank you so very much for the kind telegram which you and Mayor Wright sent to me on my selection as President of Auburn University. I am grateful for the pledge of support and the knowledge that I can count on your assistance.

I know from my experience in Florida the tremendous importance and value of having a legislator who is fully familiar with university operations. I want to assure you of my firm intentions to cooperate with you in every way possible and hope that you will feel free to call upon me at any time. I hope that I have an opportunity in the very near future to meet you personally and am looking forward to working in association with you.

With best personal wishes, I am

Sincerely yours,
Harry M. Philpott - Vice President – University of Florida

In July, Pete and several legislators visited Bryce Hospital, the state's largest psychiatric facility, and Partlow State School, the state school for the severely mentally handicapped. They heard appeals from hospital officials as they begged for help from the legislature so that help could be given to the mentally ill and handicapped. In response, Pete said, "The people of Alabama just don't know about the conditions which exist here. If they did, something would be done." He pledged to seek an early

74

conference with Gov. Wallace to discuss the needs of the hospitals. He also said he would bring the needs of the hospitals to the attention of the House Ways and Means Committee.

The first two weeks in October Pete spent at Fort Benning, Georgia, on active duty as a reserve officer. He was assigned to the G-2 (Intelligence) Section of The Infantry Center for on-the-job training in intelligence and security. Trained as a lecturer in the field of the Army's role in every-day life by the Command and General Staff College at Fort Leavenworth, Kansas, Pete was often asked to speak to civic and educational groups about the subject.

1965 - MAJORS ROBERT YORK AND PETE TURNHAM

Later in October, a long-awaited Lee County public fishing lake became a reality when Pete announced that $125,000 in federal funds would be forthcoming through the Alabama State Conservation Department to meet engineering and construction costs. According to his son, Joe, Pete originally went to the Conservation Department and was told they did not have the money for a lake. But, they told him there were counties which had been allocated money for public lakes and it was never used. If Pete could get those counties to agree to turn their money back in or give written notice they would not use the money to build a lake, Lee County could have those funds. Tenacious person that Pete is, he did just that. The site of the 131-acre lake, opened in the summer of 1968, is between Auburn and Opelika, about 10 miles from both, that site being one of the nicest and most suitable in the state, according to one of the engineers who worked on it. Pete had been pushing the project for seven years, and he hailed it as "a tremendous asset for developing the youth of the county and greatly contributing to the welfare of the adults."

In November, Pete was appointed one of five members of the Joint Interim Committee on higher education by Speaker of the House, Albert Brewer. The committee was designed to study ways in which to coordinate the efforts of Alabama's four-year colleges, junior colleges, vocational and technical schools, and private and parochial schools. And, always involved in his church and its related activities, Pete made the time to attend the dedication services of the Auburn Heights Baptist Mission.

Early 1966 brought more proposed legislation for education from Pete which included a $10 million "cushion" fund to guard against school proration and a $15 million revolving "operational" fund to be used instead of loans by schools for operational expenses in September and October before new school appropriations became available. He said it could save the state $150,000 a year in interest. And, he also proposed a 10 per cent raise in teacher and administrative staff salaries, more money for transportation services, more teachers to offset expanding enrollments, and a new state junior college in Chilton County. A student himself, in May Pete completed Unit V of the U. S. Army "National Security Management" course. In August, the $44 million emergency education appropriation package was signed by Governor Wallace. The six bills included revenue to give teachers a 10 percent boost in their state-paid salary, provided revenue to employ 1,200 new teachers, earmarked $11 million for the junior college and trade school program, and gave substantial increases in revenue to the institutions of higher learning.

At the beginning of the 1967 legislative session, Pete was, for the third time, elected chairman of the House Education Committee, and was also named again to the influential House Ways and Means Committee. The Senate and House adopted a resolution to set up a Joint Interim Committee on Finance and Taxation charged with studying, between January 18 and May 1, the financial condition of the state. Pete was appointed to serve on that committee as well. Continuing his many speaking engagements, Pete was the guest speaker at the January Auburn Kiwanis luncheon, giving his prediction of the hot issues to come before the new legislature.

As the elected chairman of the Legislative Cotton Study Committee, Pete was also active in helping Alabama cotton farmers through their most disastrous crop year in history, when it was either too wet, making ineffective the plant nutrients, herbicides, fungicides, and insecticides that were used, too dry, or too cold. In a September 14 letter from Alabama U. S. State Senator Lister Hill he told Pete:

> I regret I missed the pleasure of seeing you when you and other members of the Alabama Cotton Study Committee called by the office on yesterday. ... I have repeatedly pointed out to Agriculture Department authorities the unfairness of the current skip-row regulations to Southeastern cotton growers and will again prior to the planting of the 1967 cotton crop... I want you to know that I am continuing to work right along with my Senate colleagues in the matter. I am delighted to learn of the almost overwhelming and unanimous sentiment which has been expressed by cotton

producers to ASCS authorities at the recent series of meetings in favor of reinstating the regulations which existed prior to the rule change in 1965. ... I will leave no stone unturned in my continued efforts to remove the unfairness and inequities of the current regulations of cotton producers in Alabama and the Southeast. I would, of course, welcome any further thinking and views you may have regarding the situation.

In the editorial thoughts of one of the newspapers, titled "Turnham's Case for Better Education," Pete stated: "Until two years ago the entire Alabama Legislature was dominated by rural representation. After federal reapportionment, it changed overnight. The House, for instance, has only 33 former members back who have served before; and every vote in this body, if counties voted together, could be controlled by 9 counties. The Senate has 27 new members, and 11 counties there can control every vote if they stick together. There are 196 members of the House and 35 senators.

We can make a good case for education in Alabama, for it is education that has led our state to its greatest heights. It will be education that can continue to lead our people in the development of our natural wealth, for we have in our state 10% of the nation's natural resources, and these cannot be developed without good education.

Ninety percent of all the scientists who ever lived are alive and at work today. These scientists cannot be replaced without proper educational facilities at all levels.

Two-thirds of all the products we will buy in 1980 have not been thought of today. More change has taken place since 1918 than in all previous time since the world was created. Fifty percent of all sixth-grade students today will be working in 1989 at jobs not now in existence.

Alabama is blessed with so many good things, but our greatest asset is our people.

On the Gulf coast of our state is a large body of water, salt water, which is waiting for some well-trained minds – educated minds – to go to work on it. Scientists tell us that in this body of water there are 60 known elements of the earth – gold, silver, oil, food, salt, and an abundant supply of protein foods. Someone needs to explore, and probe into this ocean of wealth. It will take educated minds, the products of our educational system, to delve into these mysteries.

We are working on a 29-package program for education in Alabama, and while it may not be everything we need, it is a great step forward. I predict that it will pass.

If our republic ever dies, it may be due to a breakdown in our educational system. That is how important good education is to any nation.

History has shown that the historical cycle of a political body is that man progresses from bondage to spiritual faith – from spiritual faith to courage – from courage to freedom - from freedom to abundance. Then comes the warning – from abundance to selfishness – from selfishness to apathy – from apathy to dependency – and from dependency to bondage again.

In all our educational processes our people must be taught that work and learning must go hand in hand."

Alabama Contract Sales, Inc.

In 1967 Pete felt the time had come to go into business for himself. He said, "I wanted to try my luck. I didn't go into business to make money necessarily. I worked for another company and I said, 'Well, if I can do good with this company, working for somebody else, I ought to be able to do alright with my own business.'" He had never failed to make or exceed his monthly quota of sales for Marshall and Bruce, so felt he could begin to make plans to open his own business. Going into a business he felt was safe, not a situation where he had to take chances to survive, he decided to sell a commodity which would always be needed; school and office furniture. On starting the business he said, "I always wanted to do it but I didn't know how I was going to manage it. But, I knew if I kept knocking at the door it would come to me. And it did!" Building the business on the values of honesty and the importance of keeping your word, he founded Alabama Contract Sales, Inc. As news began to spread about ACS's business philosophies and products, the orders increased and Pete knew he had to expand to deliver those products. Excited about the growth of the business, Pete said, "When I made my first thousand dollars, we had a ball! Last week (in 2018) we had an order to come in that was over a million, so we've been real fortunate." According to his son, Tim, Pete had an office in his house, no secretary, and no bookkeeping system when he began. Tim said, "When I started working there in 1972, the second employee in the company, Dad had a filing cabinet with twelve folders in it, one for each month, January through December, and he had invoices in each one. He would hand write the invoices, put the carbon copy in the appropriate folder, then assume they were all paid. He was a trusting person, and was pretty much safe doing that because the business was mostly from publicly funded programs (school systems)." After traveling with Pete for a week, Tim said he came to work the following Monday and Pete said, "Go open your trunk." He did, and Pete filled it with catalogues. Then he said, "Your territory is from Birmingham north." Tim said okay, headed out, and traveled every week for years. When Tim joined the business they primarily sold classroom furniture, furnished by a company out of Conway, Arkansas, called Virco. One day the area rep came into the office and said the company had decided to go direct, which would eliminate all the dealers in the country, and on an exclusive basis. Tim said, "There we were with nothing on the wagon to sell, so we started adding and diversifying, making sure, if that happened again, it would not affect us dramatically."

People, especially the competition, felt it was a big advantage for Pete to be in the legislature and to be selling to state entities which were funded by the legislature, but, according to Tim, "It was really the other way around. People were afraid to do business with us because of the criticism." Ever the striver, Pete said, "The more people you contacted, the more you were going to sell," and he and Tim continued to reach out and expand, evolving through the years. Today, the biggest product offering is Spectator Seating Systems, which involves telescopic and fixed seating in high school gymnasiums and stadiums. They sell them in Alabama, the panhandle of Florida, and the gulf of Mississippi, about 65% of the market. Per Tim, "We also sell laboratory casework furniture, which is science and technology furniture for biology and chemistry labs in high schools and universities, and we sell dormitory furniture and media furniture. We sell pretty much anything that goes into K through 12 and university settings, along with office furniture for public buildings."

In the early years everything was done by bids. It still is today, but now there are state contracts, and a tremendous amount of work goes into those. Pete said, "When a company is ready to build a building, we draw their plans and specs, and it is wonderful. It helps them and us, too. When people find out you can help them with no obligation, they come to you and let you do a lot of work." Per Tim, "Where a new school is being built, we have to do computer assisted drawings, space planning, and interior design services." From a one man company begun in 1967 to a two man company five years later, Tim said, "We're not big, but we have grown from $240,000 gross sales in that year (1967) to where we are today, which is quite a few zeros beyond that."

According to Tim, Pete ran the business, cared about it, and was always giving. One time a minister called, the church had placed an order, and he told Pete the church was really struggling financially, so Pete said to Tim, "Let's just sell it to them for cost." Tim suggested, instead, they give them a good deal on the order, ever mindful of Pete's giving nature, and what it takes to run a business. Another time a good friend, Bill Becket, was actively involved in helping the Alabama Sheriff's Girls Ranch in Camp Hill. According to Tim, "They were building a welcome center there, raising a lot of money, and he came to us and asked if we would be willing to donate the furniture for it. Pete said 'Absolutely'! Dad wanted to help people, even in business, and he did."

Pete and Tim sold the business in December 2016, with Tim agreeing to stay another two years to help with the transition. At that time there were ten employees, with the installation work subbed out to five different companies. Those companies had around 100 employees who unloaded the trucks, put together the items, and did the installation process. Rebecca Dowdy, who was hired in 1996 after her graduation from Auburn in Interior Design, is now one of the owners and has remained close to Pete as a good friend.

On the company website "About Us" page the last paragraph tells the story of the business today. "Our customers consist of school superintendents, architects, designers, general contractors, and private companies. We represent nearly 100 manufacturers, many on State Contract, enabling ACS to offer the best solution for your particular project. As always, if we do not offer the best solution we exhaust our knowledge and resources to help find you a company which does offer you the best solution. We understand we are in a service industry and if we do not earn your repeat business we will be out of business! Our team has over 200 years of combined knowledge and expertise. Please contact our company and give us the opportunity to demonstrate why over 90% of our customers are repeat customers!"

Continuing To Serve

*I*n April 1968 at their annual meeting, that year in Arkansas, Pete was elected Treasurer of the Southern Interstate Nuclear Board. In a letter to Pete dated October 10, 1968, Governor Albert P. Brewer said: *"As an admirer of your personal accomplishments in the legislature, I know that you will render an outstanding service as treasurer for the SINB."*

Continuing his busy speaking schedule, Pete addressed the Elmore County High School FFA banquet on April 26th, and on May 16th he gave the address at the Gamma Sigma Delta banquet in Auburn. Later in the year he addressed the Wadley Kiwanis Club, calling attention to the difficult problems facing the state and nation. He stated that these could be solved only through honesty, integrity, and hard work, and the Kiwanians left feeling that "these qualities were found in the speaker in a superlative degree." Pete said that the present struggle in the legislature was a power struggle between the large and small counties, and he called attention to the fact that federal interference was in large measure the cause of the struggle.

PETE AND HIS DAD, J. HENRY

Among the problems were education, highway construction, law observance, pollution, and pornography. As had often happened before when Pete spoke, his proud dad, Henry, was present at the meeting.

On Sunday, August 25, 1968, Pete and Kay were feted at a beautiful and very special reception in the fellowship hall of their church, Lakeview Baptist, on the

KAY AND PETE WITH CHILDREN DIANE, TIM, RUTHMARY, JOE AND GRANDDAUGHTER, AUDREY

occasion of their 25th wedding anniversary. Hosts were their children, Diane, Tim, Ruthmary, and Joe. Guests were friends from First Baptist Church, Lakeview Baptist Church, Auburn, Opelika, and Tuskegee. It was a time for family and friends to honor two people who were examples of love, hard work, and devotion to each other, their family, their friends, and to their community.

Pete had been instrumental in pushing in the legislature for funds to build an Alabama Pesticide Laboratory at Auburn, and in 1969 the building became a reality.

SECOND FROM LEFT - FLOYD COOK, VP; JIMMY THOMPSON, CAFFCO PRESIDENT; AND PETE, STOCKHOLDER - OTHER NAMES UNKNOWN

One of Pete's Auburn roommates, Jimmy Thompson (James Lamar, Sr.), opened a florist, Capital Floral Company, in 1950, later to become CAFFCO International, a corporation encompassing retail, wholesale distribution, importing, international trading, and Asian manufacturing, distributing home decor, gifts, and holiday products. At Jimmy's invitation, Pete became a stockholder as CAFFCO International was being developed, and was on the board of directors for twenty years. The factories producing the products were established in China, with some business being done in Japan, and Pete and Vice President of the company, Floyd Cook, made a trip to Japan and Hong Kong (to become the CAFFCO headquarters) with Jimmy in early 1969 as the first factory was being built.

Speaking to the Opelika Rotarians early in 1969, Pete said there would be an announcement soon regarding the location of a large plant in that area of the state saying, "This area is the most sought-after section of the state." Covering several topics, he said, "One of the first bills we face as we resume legislative sessions will be one to legalize tandem trailers on Alabama's highways," stating Alabama's interstate system was about two-thirds complete. Other problems included mental health and parks and recreation. Plans were in the making to build four centers to help train mentally handicapped children and thirteen comprehensive mental health centers across the state. A $43 million bond issue was approved for parks and recreation two years prior in an effort to enable the state to capture a larger share of the tourist dollar. Some of the results of the recent special session for education included legislation providing for the election of state board members and appointment of a state superintendent, a commission on higher education, a continuing study committee on public education, and higher teacher salaries.

In May, a bill co-sponsored by Pete and very near and dear to his heart was passed "to establish the Alabama Commission of Higher Education for the general purpose of promoting an educational system that will provide the highest possible quality of collegiate and university education to all persons in the state able and willing to profit from it; to provide through the Commission for continuous study, analyses, evaluation, planning, reporting and recommendations for long-range planning with established priorities on a state-wide basis to assure a sound, vigorous progressive and coordinated system of higher education for this state."

In August, a fierce liquor fight was waged in the House before finally concurring 47- 46 in Senate amendments on a local option bill. The bill, allowing 16 dry counties to vote wet, was vehemently opposed by Pete. At one point he said, "We've defeated this bill, resurrected it, and passed it! The Senate knocked it around and they were probably more confused than on any other bill. The church-going people and the people with children will be involved. They're concerned about law enforcement if this passes. Let's don't let tax dollars get in our eyes! If this passes we're going to pit city against county. Economic conditions are going to change immediately." Pete's county was wet but he added, "I represent 67 counties and I've been getting mail against this from everywhere." A hard fought battle, but the bill was passed. Also in August, Pete helped sponsor a bill to provide for organizing industrial development corporations in Alabama, a boost to the growth of the economy in both the state and locally.

Mr. Pete

In October, Pete inspected the new Alabama Pesticide Laboratory after pushing the legislation to establish it. The Farm Bureau coordinated the efforts of agriculture, industry, health, conservation, and other interests in working out a pesticides testing program all could support. Later that month, Pete addressed the Auburn Lions Club on the recently concluded session of the State Legislature, assuring his fellow Lions that "in spite of all the bad publicity many worthwhile accomplishments were realized."

Herb, Pete, and Auburn

⎯⎬⎬◎

Herb White, Director of University Relations at Auburn University from 1969 to 1993, began working with that office in 1965, and he said, "Pete had been in the legislature for a good while when I started getting involved in it, and he was a tremendous help to me. He is a good friend. He was the Chairman of the Education Committee in the House for many years and was considered 'Mr. Education' by members of the legislature. He was also on the Ways and Means Committee, which is the money committee of the legislature. We were always interested in the appropriations we got from the legislature, so he and I collaborated a lot, and he was a staunch supporter of the university for all the time he was in the legislature. If there was something we wanted to do he wanted to roll up his sleeves and get enthusiastic about it and get things going! I told him one time that we wanted to do something. This was when George Wallace was governor and Governor Wallace called Pete, Peedro. We went to see Governor Wallace about this matter, and Pete just about had to sign off on me for the legislature to pass something like that because Wallace had control of the legislature. Governor Wallace said, 'Peedro, if you want this for Auburn, you know you can get it from me.' That constituted a commitment from the governor. Pete had to remind him of it several times, but we finally got it."

"One time, years ago, Pete and Kay invited my wife and me to go to eat with them at Saugahatchee Country Club. They picked us up at our house and we drove out together and had a delightful meal at the country club. As we were headed back, Pete said, 'Do you mind if I stop by the funeral home for a few minutes and speak to this family? I need to do that.' I said, 'Pete, why don't you just drop us by our house and we'll get out of your way?' He said, 'No, we're right on the way to the funeral home. Let's just stop for a minute, you can stay in the car if you want to, and I'll just run in.' We got to the funeral home and parked and I said, ' Well, Pete, we'll see you when you get back.' Then he said, 'Oh, no, no, no. I want you to go in there with me.' My wife absolutely refused to go, and Kay didn't go either. He grabbed me and we went in. There was a huge crowd of people, I didn't know a soul, and we got in line to view the remains. It must have taken 30 minutes or more to do, and he was speaking to everybody. He knew everybody and wanted to talk with them, and I wanted to drag him out of the way and get going. We finally got through, got in the car, and came home. It was a delightful occasion, but the moral of that story is, if you go out with Pete, take your own car, because no telling what's going to happen to you before you get home!"

"Another personal story about Pete... I have four daughters, and when they were in school, they shared a car. One of them, Jenny, was driving down the street one day in front of Pete's house, just around the corner from us. She felt something wobbling, stopped on the side of the road, and it turned out to be a flat tire. She didn't know what in the world she was going to do about it, because she didn't want to call me and take me away from work. Pete came running out of his house; you know how enthusiastic he is about everything and everybody. He told her not to worry about it because he could change that tire. So, there he was, a member of the state legislature and leading citizen of Auburn and Lee County, fixing a tire for this 16 or 17-year-old. She, of course, has never forgotten that, and anytime the name of Pete Turnham comes up she is enthusiastic and wants to say something nice about that wonderful person who changed that tire for her. That's the kind of guy Pete is. He's always trying to do things for people. He really enjoys doing things for people, and that's one way he got elected to the House for so many consecutive terms, and he became known as the Dean of the Alabama Legislature. He made friends wherever he went. That's one reason his business was so successful over the years. He made a lot of contacts because of his service in the legislature, he was a good person on top of that, and he was a good businessman."

1995 - AT HERB'S DAUGHTER'S WEDDING
LEFT TO RIGHT - DAVID WHITE, TAYLOR LITTLETON, HERB WHITE, ED HOBBS AND PETE

"I don't know many people like Pete Turnham. He is a rare individual and a rare member of the legislature, because he is a man of high integrity, a religious person, and he and I got along very well. He went out of his way on many occasions to help the university, to make things better for not only Auburn, but for all the people he represented."

"Back in the days that the state passed the bond issues, they would usually give Auburn ten or fifteen million dollars and we would stretch it as far as it would go. One time in particular, they had a bond issue for medical purposes, primarily pushed by the medical program in Birmingham, the University of Alabama medical program. Of course, the only thing we had that was strictly medicine was veterinary medicine, but vet medicine was not included in the bond issue, it was for human medicine. But, we did have a pharmacy school. We got with Pete and one thing led to another, and we finally got our toe in the door and got, I think it was, four million dollars or so for a new pharmacy building which was built many years ago now. It's been remodeled, and might have been rebuilt since then. Anytime we built a building like Haley Center (Education), the ten story building on the campus, and the old coliseum, that money came from the legislature. Pete had a hand in all that construction because he was on the committee the money had to come through, the Ways and Means Committee, and he was a staunch political supporter in the construction of all those buildings. Now the state does not have that. They can't afford it. Alabama keeps bragging about being the least taxed state in the union. That, on the one hand, is good for people who are retiring and moving from state to state. But, as far as progress in the state is concerned, it's a very short-sighted view. Taxes are certainly not unimportant, but you advocate a tax and you're hard pressed to win the next election. So, everybody is against taxes. But, it's a case of Alabama being the least taxed state in the union, or close to that, and it's not been a good thing for education, or anything else…mental health, the roads, bridges, infrastructure. They are talking about a bond issue now, so, hopefully they will do something like that. The money for education has just not increased that much in our state. Hopefully, one of these days, we'll get a situation where the electorate is a little bit further advanced than the attitude of no new taxes."

About the university soliciting funds… "We would usually have a meeting at the university, and the president and the people in control of things would talk to Pete, other members of the legislature from around here, and those alumni legislators who would come, about what our needs and objectives were. Part of my job was not to formulate that policy, but to try to help carry it out once it got to Montgomery. So, I played that role and kept Pete reminded of lots of different things that would come up in the legislature. Of course, we were interested in one narrow approach to the situation, so I was involved in all that. It was just a small part of what a legislator has to contend with. Pete was the main supporter we had in the legislature, even though we had a number of those in the Senate at that time. But the bills originate in the House, sometimes coming from the governor's recommendation."

Election Time Again

It was time for another election and Pete ran for his seat in the House again. Because of a reapportionment in 1965, he had the following explanation put on his campaign literature.

FOR EDUCATION—INDUSTRY—AGRICULTURE

VOTE AND WORK FOR

PETE TURNHAM

FOR

HOUSE OF REPRESENTATIVES

LEE COUNTY

RE-ELECT - -
PETE TURNHAM

Pete has served three terms in the Alabama Legislature and has worked his way to the top in Committee Assignments. He is running on a record of honesty, hard work and experience. OUR COUNTY needs Pete. Pete needs YOU.

Subject to Democratic Primary May 5, 1970

Pd. Pol. Adv. by Pete Turnham, Auburn, Ala.

(Over)

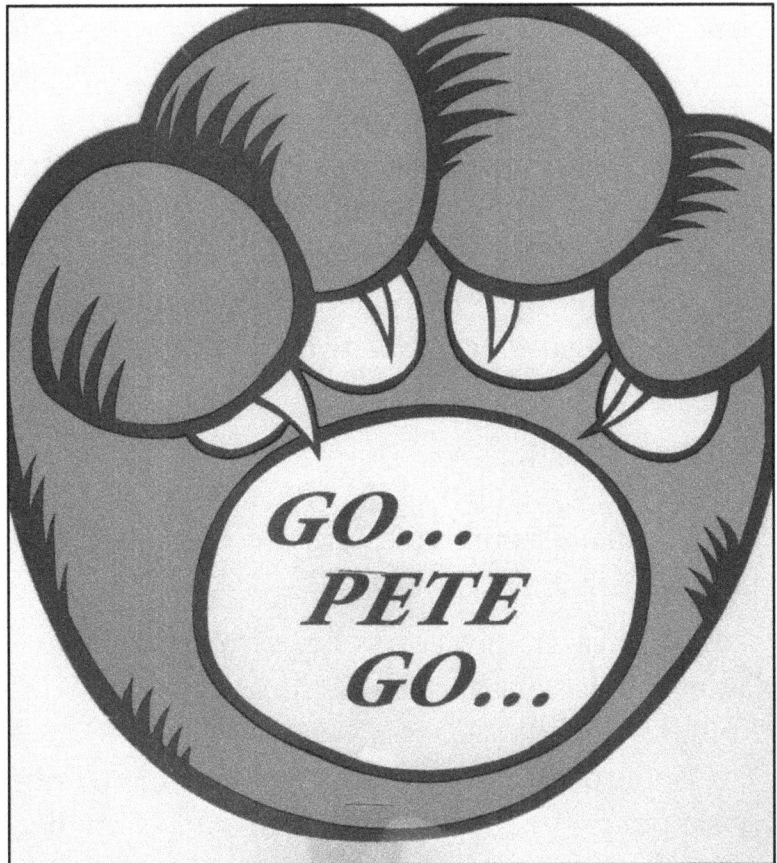

When the Alabama House of Representatives was reapportioned during 1965, the 32nd House District, composed of Lee and Russell Counties, was formed. Under the reapportionment law, the 32nd District was given 3 members of the House, to be known as Places 1, 2, and 3. Any person from either county could run for any one of these three seats.

To insure that each county will have at least one Democratic Nominee in the general election this fall, the Democratic Executive Committees of the two counties agreed that in the Democratic Primary, Place 1 will be a permanent seat that goes to Russell County; Place 2 will be a permanent seat for Lee County; and Place 3 will be a "swing" seat. Lee County would have this seat for four years and then the seat would go to Russell County for the next four years. All three candidates must run in both Lee and Russell Counties. I now hold Place 2, the permanent seat, and am running for re-election. Although the arrangement designates Places 1 and 2 for certain counties, candidates for these places, as well as those for Place 3, must run in both counties.

Some of his qualifications appearing on the literature were:

*Served in the Alabama House of Representatives since 1959; served with four governors. *Supported highway projects: 4-laning of U.S. 280 and 431, and I-85 interstate. *Voted and worked for improved educational program and industrial development. *Sponsored largest bond issue for schools in the history of Alabama. Over 15 million dollars came to Lee and Russell Counties from this program. *Sponsored Voluntary Admissions Bill for Mental Health. *Worked for development of Phenix City Docks and Grain Elevator. *Worked for Public Lake for our area. This lake will be open for fishing in June. *Worked for Mental Health Center, Trade School, and Clinic for Alcoholics for our area. *Married, 4 children, Businessman, Baptist Deacon and Sunday school teacher.

Elected again, Pete began serving his second term as Chairman of the Education Committee, a member of the House Ways and Means Committee, a member of the Military Affairs Committee, and was appointed a member of the Education Commission of the States.

Always eager to serve in his own church as well as others, Pete gave the Sunday evening message, titled "Education and Politics," at the Mt. Zion Methodist Church in Smiths, Alabama, on April 12, 1970. In the bulletin it was stated that Pete "sponsored the bill which was considered one of the most important pieces of legislation in the history of Alabama, a 116 million dollar package for new and improved buildings and equipment. Many trade schools and junior colleges were built with this money also. Pete also sponsored a bill that appropriated $250,000.00 to build a pesticide laboratory at Auburn to help analyze feeds and foods for possible harmful materials. Other legislation he has sponsored includes mental health and industrial development programs."

In May 1971, there seemed to be a somewhat half-hearted effort in the Legislature to move the Auburn School of Pharmacy from the Auburn campus to the Auburn University Montgomery (AUM) campus. With the urging of many Auburn

1970- AT A PRESENTATION IN
GOV. ALBERT BREWER'S OFFICE

pharmacy graduates, the Lee County Hospital, the Auburn and Opelika Chambers of Commerce, and other governing bodies of the two cities, Pete argued convincingly that the School of Pharmacy should stay in Auburn, and it did. There was also an 11th hour approval of a $53 million medical education bond issue package passed by the Senate, which included a $4 million grant, mentioned above, for expansion to the university's School of Pharmacy.

There were five Acts which Pete sponsored in the 1971 legislative session having

to do with law enforcement, the Lee County Schools Superintendent, and county expenses and compensations. All of them passed. Act 73 provided deputies and assistants for the sheriff of Lee County. The Act provided for the appointment of the county superintendent of education of Lee County by the county board of education. Act 75 was an act to apply in counties having populations of not less than 49,000 nor more than 50,000, providing for payment of expense allowances for the deputy or county solicitors of those counties from the county treasury. Act 76 was to fix the compensation of the sheriffs of all counties having populations of not less than 60,000 or more than 65,000 according to the most recent federal decennial census. Act 77 amended the Act which regulated further the office of sheriff in the state, and prescribed the annual salaries of sheriffs of the several counties classified on a population basis.

In July, Pete attended, in Boston, the annual meeting of the Education Commission of the States, and was re-elected to the Steering Committee, the organization's policy-making body responsible for decisions made between annual meetings. A non-profit organization, the Education Commission of the States, was formed to improve communication and encourage working relationships among state governors, legislators, and educators for the improvement of education.

1971 - GOV. GEORGE WALLACE ADDRESSING THE LEGISLATURE PETE IN FRONT OF US FLAG

In August, Pete successfully fought a bill to legalize dog racing and pari-mutuel betting in any Alabama county that wanted it. He warned his legislative colleagues, saying, "Vote for the bill and then go back home and try to run again." If the bill had passed, one half of the proceeds would have been earmarked for education and the other half for mental health, but Pete felt strongly it was not something which would be good for Alabama, saying dog racing would bring into the state "elements you never heard of."

In December, as the current President of the Alabama Association for Mental Health, Pete was the guest speaker at the annual Mobile County Association of Mental Health. He told the group, "The major challenge to the Mental Health Association in the nation today is to weld itself into a single family including state, chapter, and national levels. Each should have its own area of responsibility and each should respect areas of responsibility of the others. But, as a single unit called, 'The Mental Health Association', we, the volunteers, can move this important health endeavor forward."

Early in the new year Pete received a letter, dated January 3, 1972, stating: *I want to thank you for your part, which was considerable, in getting an increase in retirement benefits for teachers. This increase was reflected in my check for December, which I received yesterday. The change from 1¼% to 1¾% was more than I had expected. I believe it was your efforts in the special session which were responsible for the favorable legislation. I hope that never again will it be necessary to oppose a diversion of teacher retirement funds for other purposes, worthy as they may be.*

In February, during a special session of the Legislature, House Bill 300, co-sponsored by Pete, to change the tax figures back to 30-25-20 for three classifications of property, was killed. Pete deplored the lack of action on the part of the Senate and stated that it could ruin the county for all property except utilities to be taxed at the 15 % level. "Failure of the Senate to pass House Bill 300 can wreck the cities of Opelika and Auburn, Lee County, and the three school systems because use of the 15 per cent figure will cost them several hundred thousand dollars. Our county school system is crying for help at the present time. It is sad for a progressive county such as Lee to go backward instead of forward in this matter. It is a legislative matter and should have been done by the Legislature. The House faced up to its responsibility in this matter and passed the needed legislation, but the Senate refused to act on it."

In October 1972 it was announced that a request for a $2 million building to replace the outdated 56-year-old facility that housed the state's Veterinary Diagnostic and Brucellosis Laboratory on the Auburn University campus was being prepared for approval by the next session of the state legislature. Pete was the author of the bill and said, "It is a much overdue thing and a facility that must be kept up to date if it is to provide the proper service to our poultry and livestock producers. We are going to try to get the bill in early and get it passed just as quickly as it is possible." The laboratory had recently been in the news when the state was called on to handle the largest vaccination program in its history involving Alabama horses and mules. In spite of its cramped quarters it handled sleeping sickness vaccine for thousands of horses and mules and was said to have had one of the best operated programs in the nation.

In January 1973 Pete attended the National Forum of State Legislators on Older Americans in Washington, D. C. The 160 delegates felt they left the forum with a greater awareness of problems facing the aging and a better understanding of how to begin searching for effective solutions. And they also agreed that much of the red tape involved in implementing Federal programs for the aging could be alleviated by dealing with problems of the elderly at local and state levels. At the end of the forum Pete said, "In my judgment, this meeting was the best that could have been planned for legislators at the state level. It gives me the background to go back home and plan state programs that will blend with Federal projects. Too many times we have depended on the Federal government to handle programs for our older Americans. All of us at the state level must take more of an active part in the general well being of the elderly. A program like this at least every two years would be invaluable in keeping state legislators abreast of current trends and opportunities for all older Americans."

Just prior to the convening of the Legislature's 1973 regular biennial session, Pete spoke about the topics to be addressed. Those included a $1,000 increase in pay for school teachers, appropriations to cover Auburn University basic requests, including $5 million for relocation of the main facilities of the Agricultural Experiment Station, and approval of legislative reapportionment before the May 17 deadline set by the U. S. Middle District Court. Also, full legal status for 18-year-olds, significantly increased expenditures for mental health facilities, revamping of the Pensions and Security (Welfare) Department and prison systems, and some kind of relief for the county school system would be on the agenda. And, perhaps most importantly to voters, no new taxes would be discussed. Pete said, "We've been adding programs from the Special Education Trust Fund without any new taxes, and this can't go on forever. It would probably be better to add a small increase a little at a time instead of a big increase all at one time. But I find absolutely no sentiment of any kind for a tax increase at this session. This is the last session before the legislators are up for re-election next spring, and nobody wants to run with a tax increase fresh on the voters' minds."

As Chairman of the House Education Committee, Pete was mindful of the fact his major battle would be over appropriations for education. Auburn University was a major part of his constituency and at the same time he had to tend to the needs of the public schools. And, as a member of the Ways and Means committee he would be part of considering the commission's report on education and then presenting a budget. "I'm not splitting the money on any percentage basis," Pete said. "The commission's report is all for all in a way because we'll rewrite the recommendations in the Ways and Means committee. We'll present a budget which I think will take care of public schools and higher education. I'm going to take the lead to get extra money that Auburn University feels it needs. Auburn has a good name all over the state and most legislators are sympathetic to the problems of the University. I think we have assurances from them that most of the special requests from Auburn will be approved. At the same time, we'll pass a $1,000 increase for school teachers. You want to please both groups, public schools and higher education, and in most cases you can work out a compromise that won't hurt either group."

One of Pete's proudest moments was in 1973 when he authored the bill to establish a pilot kindergarten program for Alabama, which began operating in Auburn the following year. Through the years, he has enjoyed saying he ran his own wife out of business, as Kay had run her private kindergarten for years. But, public kindergarten had been a dream of both Pete and Kay for many years.

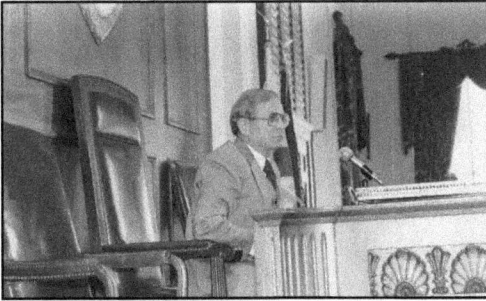
PETE PRESIDING IN THE HOUSE

That same year Pete was instrumental in the passage of the education bond issue which provided a prorated share for the three public school systems in Lee County and about $10 million to renovate an experiment station at Auburn and build a new building for the School of Architecture. He also spearheaded a bill that provided funds for a new state chemical and diagnostic laboratory to be built on the Auburn campus.

Pete stayed close to his constituency, ever mindful of their wants and needs. He said, "It's always been my nature to stay close to people. I go out to meet the public several times a week. Last week I spoke to three different groups in one day. I talk to civic groups, church groups, go to family reunions and picnics, visit the hospital, go to funerals, meet people on the street. It's a good way to get people's ideas. I make all the barbecues and horse shows and cow shows I can, but they can't get away with kidding me about it being an election year because I'm there every year. I won't ever judge another beauty contest though. It's bad politics. You make 25 families mad and one happy. I did it once, but that's all."

"You run into more special interest groups in this county than you do in the average rural county. You've got more retired people and you've got student groups that are interested in things like pollution. Lee County is a heavy letter-writing county. I got 500 letters on one issue during a session of the legislature and it's not unusual to get up to 150 a week. I probably get 20 – 30 calls a day, more than that when the legislature is in session."

"Staying in touch with the people and carrying out their requests is the key. You can please 95 per cent of them. But, there's a tough five per cent that's hard to handle."

A lot of the calls and letters were requests to find people jobs, have someone admitted to the state mental hospital, or get someone out of jail, which is one thing he could not do. He said the constant calls and duties he performed were tough on his family, but he liked the life. "I enjoy it thoroughly. It's amazing how few people know how to get something done in Montgomery, and it gives me a lot of personal satisfaction to serve them in a way they really need help. You need to be very frank and honest, not lead people to believe something can be done and then not do it. A

97

surprise is better than a shock. It's hard for people to trust politicians, but I think I've overcome that with the majority of people. My first year I promised a lot of things I thought I could do but couldn't. It took me a long time to realize what was possible. Fortunately, people here are very considerate of politicians."

Entering the computer age, Pete sponsored Act 372 in 1973 which authorized the governing bodies of counties with not less than 60,000 nor more than 65,000 to provide a computer operator to serve all county offices and to be paid from the general funds of those counties.

One of Pete's greatest joys in 1973 was escorting his daughter, Ruthmary, in the pageant where she was crowned Miss Judson College.

PETE ESCORTING DAUGHTER RUTHMARY

Grandchildren & Great-Grandchildren

4 GENERATIONS - PETE AND KAY, (DAUGHTER) DIANE AND BILL, (GRANDDAUGHTER) AUDREY, (GREAT-GRANDCHILDREN) AUSTIN, SARAH (KATHRYN), NOAH, AND APRIL

60TH WEDDING ANNIVERSARY – PETE AND KAY WITH GRANDCHILDREN ABBY, PETE (MATTHEW), TIMOTHY, AND BLAKE (BENTON)

3 GENERATIONS – PETE, (SON) TIM, (GRANDSONS) BLAKE AND TIMOTHY

3 GENERATIONS – PETE, (SON) JOE, (GRANDSON) PETE

PETE AND KAY WITH
GREAT-GRANDDAUGHTER, SARAH

PETE WITH GRANDDAUGHTER, AUDREY,
WHO SERVED AS A PAGE IN THE HOUSE

PETE AND GRANDSON, BLAKE

PETE AND GRANDSON, TIMOTHY

PETE AND GRANDSON, PETE

PETE AND GRANDDAUGHTER, ABBY

PETE'S GREAT-GRANDCHILDREN,
LAUREN AND DREW

JOE, TIM HOLDING GRANDDAUGHTER,
LAUREN, AND PETE

PETE AND GRANDSON, TIMOTHY

GRANDCHILDREN, LINDSEY, BLAKE,
TIMOTHY, ABBY, AND PETE

PETE AND GREAT-GRANDDAUGHTER LAUREN

GRANDDAUGHTERS JENNY AND AUDREY

Ted, Pete, and The Legislature

As Pete prepared his campaign in 1973 for his fifth term in the House, which now included Auburn, Loachapoka, Roxana, Waverly, Camp Hill, and part of Chambers County, Ted Little was preparing his campaign to run for the position of Alabama State Senator, representing Tallapoosa, Chambers (the county where Pete was raised), Lee (the county Pete represented), and Randolph Counties. Both won their elections and Ted said, "Pete was a seasoned member of the legislature already and was a great help to me. I was a green freshman and did not know beans about the Alabama legislature but for the fact that I had the strong hand of a person like Pete Turnham to tell me, 'Ted, this is what we're doing in the House, this is what ya'll are going to be doing in the Senate, and this is what you are going to be needing to do for mine and your district.' Pete, as a politician, was damn good. Pete was a natural."

1973 - PETE CONGRATULATES TED ON WINNING THE PRIMARY

"Pete always gave me some good lessons about who to see and who to see but not be seen with. He knew enough about politics to say, 'Now, if you see this person over here he can help you. But, if these people over here see you with this person, it's not going to help you. So, when you see this person over here, you keep that person there, then you go with these people over here, and don't tell them who you last visited.'"

Pete has always been known for attending weddings, funerals, and other milestone occasions for family, friends, co-workers, and acquaintances. "I used to say, Pete, do you ever send flowers to a funeral? He'd say, 'No, I go to the funeral.' And he did. Pete went all over the state for his business AND funerals."

"One day I was going to the barbershop. Pete said, 'Now, Ted, you know how to deal with the folks in Auburn, don't you?' I said, 'Pete, I don't know that I do, the right way.' He said, 'Any time you see anybody in downtown Auburn who has on a shirt and tie, and maybe a coat, you say, 'Professor, how are you doing?' You don't know who he is, but he thinks you do, and 99% of the time you'll be right. It will be someone associated with the college.' That was a good rule of thumb for politicking in Auburn."

Ted said Pete has a unique way of knowing how to pose for a picture. "He knows how to cock his head. He is photogenic anyway, and the camera always picks him up well. It is a gift he has, he knows when to turn it on, and he is a master at doing it."

One of the first big meetings in which Ted was involved, along with all the other constituents from his area, was with Gov. Wallace in his office, and it provided a moment Ted thought was comical. Pete had not been voting well with the governor lately, and, per Ted, there was nothing wrong with that. Ted said, "Sometimes you vote with the governor, sometimes you don't. As we were walking in, the governor was greeting us, 'Senator Little, how are you doing?, etc.' When Pete walked in the governor said, 'Oh, we now have Pete coming in.' It brought a coolness to the room. It was the wit of George Wallace and the way Pete Turnham knew how to handle the situation, and he took it in great stride. That's just politics."

"Pete's accomplishments in the legislature were huge. He obviously was a front-runner in beginning to get the state to wake up and see that supporting higher education had to be the future of Alabama. He was very able to keep Auburn's budget in line with the University of Alabama's budget, which was extremely important. One thing about Auburn that Pete knew well was that every county had a county extension office, and in that office was an agent. Pete knew every one of them. If Pete was trying to get a certain number of votes on an issue he was interested in and a county was not cooperating, Pete would call the county agent and say, 'Can you give me a little help with your house member? I need your vote.' Phone calls would take place and a fellow would say, 'Pete, I've thought about this situation, and I'm now going to vote with you.'"

"Pete is certainly known for vocational education and the kindergarten program. He is probably one major reason Lyman Ward Military Academy in Camp Hill is still in existence today. It was tough times for private schools, especially those that had to charge a lot for tuition, and Pete won an appropriation from the state for the school; and, that

1975 - LEFT TO RIGHT - TED LITTLE, WENDELL MITCHELL, BO TORBERT, DICK OWEN, AND PETE TURNHAM

does not happen often with taxpayer dollars. I give him a lot of credit for being such a strong advocate for Lyman Ward."

"Pete knew how to speak well from the podium, the 'well' of the House. He has a strong voice and it would echo well. He would make his points and was respectful to the presiding officer. When he chaired the Education Committee in the House for years, he was a very capable committee chairman."

"Pete was always a gentleman. Like it says in the movie, he was 'An Officer and a Gentleman.'"

Continuing to Expand
Duties and Responsibilities

~∰⊙

At the first session of the legislature in 1974, beginning his fifth term, Pete was again elected Chairman of the Education Committee and was returned to membership on the powerful House Ways and Means Committee.

Able to help support both religion and education, Pete was the master of ceremonies in May of 1974 at the kick-off dinner for the first ever Judson College $1.5 million capital gifts campaign. He was a strong supporter and general chairman of the campaign for the Auburn-Opelika area. At the event, Judson President N. H. McCrummen said, "In recent years, when many colleges have been experiencing great difficulty in balancing budgets, Judson has been able to keep a balanced operating budget with the help of the Alabama Baptist State Convention."

1974 also brought sadness for Pete with the death of his brother, Tobe, in July.

In a special session called in early 1975, Pete asked Governor Wallace to propose raising the interest rates which banks were allowed to charge on money loaned to customers, a proposal Governor Wallace endorsed. Wallace asked the legislature to approve the removal of the current 6 per cent maximum interest rate which the state could collect on its $300 million in bank deposits. Pete, asking to raise the interest rate to around 10%, said it would ease the burden on the bankers, realtors, and lending institutions, saying banks, in some instances, could not make large loans because the interest they would have to pay to get the money would exceed the 8 per cent they were allowed by state law to charge the borrower. "Carpenters, brick masons, and people in that category are out of work in this country because people can't get the money to build new homes," Pete said. The proposed bill would "have a tremendously good effect on the economy of Alabama and would shake loose the home building money for the depressed home building industry in the state. The banks and savings and loan associations cannot lend money at 8 per cent to Alabama residents for building homes when they can send the money out of state and get a much higher return on their investment."

One of Pete's earliest actions in the 1975 legislative session was to sponsor a resolution to form a study committee on a uniform system for reporting and investigating deaths in Alabama, honoring a request from the State Toxicology Lab, which hoped to provide more reliable reports on the cause of deaths.

In March of 1975, Pete helped support the request made by Auburn President Harry M. Philpott for total main campus appropriations totaling a 63.3 per cent increase, $45.7 million in 1976 and $49.7 in 1977.

In April, at the annual meeting in Kansas City, Missouri, of the Southern Interstate Nuclear Board, as mentioned previously, Pete was elected to his first term as president of the organization, the first Alabamian to hold the office. Also, in this position, Pete attended the Southern Governors' Conference in Orlando, Florida in September, where he delivered a report on education to the members.

On May 30, Pete proudly returned to Milltown to his alma mater, Chambers County High School, as the commencement speaker. In his address, he challenged the graduates to use some of Alabama's higher education institutions to further their own training.

In June, as the legislative year was coming to an end, Pete had to fight hard, maybe his toughest floor fight in his legislative career, to get his state kindergarten bill passed. He began the session by introducing a bill that would give free tuition to those over 65 years of age at state institutions, but that bill did not pass. Then, he introduced the bill that would allow local school systems to initiate a kindergarten program, following the program he introduced and which was passed in 1973 to have a pilot program in each of the old eight congressional districts. Amendment after amendment was introduced to gut the bill, but Pete successfully managed to beat them down and when the final vote came, the bill was passed.

Another bill Pete introduced was to provide assistance to families with dependents in mental institutions outside Alabama. "Alabama doesn't have facilities to care for some special problems," Pete said, "and can't afford to set up special institutions at this time." The bill gave families in need of facilities outside the state the same daily allowance allotted by the state for dependents in Alabama mental institutions. In a talk with members of the War Eagle Lions Club he pointed out that support of mental health programs was something everyone should take part in. Pointing out that the American Medical Association had declared that treating emotional illnesses was America's most pressing medical need, Pete cited some steps taken by state administrative and legislative action. He pointed specifically to the raising of patient expenditure from $2.50 per day a few years earlier to the present $12.50. He also said a patient could now volunteer for treatment at a state facility and money was being hunted to help pay for needed medications after a patient was released. Pete said he saw emotional problems as just another form of treatable illness and said the public could help by supporting mental health programs and erasing the stigma associated with treatment for a mental problem. In appreciation for all Pete had been and was doing for mental health in Alabama, he had recently received the first Silver Award for outstanding work in mental health from the Alabama Association of Community Mental Health Centers, particularly acknowledging his sponsorship of Act 310 which set up community mental health centers in the state.

Other bills Pete co-sponsored during the busy legislative year were to provide for the licensing of speech pathologists and audiologists, to require persons to stop their vehicles when approaching church buses loading and unloading passengers, to establish credit for military service for retiring teachers, and, with a passionate plea, to upgrade the Alabama prisons, saying they are "the most dangerous place in the world today."

In October Pete went to Poland as part of an educational study tour, sponsored by the National Institute for Educational Leadership in cooperation with George Washington University. He represented the South as one of 20 government policy-makers to see how vocational, early, and higher education functioned in Poland and to exchange ideas with educational leaders there. On a postcard he sent to Kay he said, *"Everything is going well and we were received by the Minister of Education and staff today. Our Embassy Staff is very helpful. We go to Krakow tomorrow. The people are friendly."* Dr. William Gill, director of the National Tillage Machinery Laboratory and adjunct professor of agricultural engineering at Auburn had two ongoing research projects in Poland at the time, and he and Pete collaborated about those projects and Pete's educational objectives often before Pete's trip.

Bobby, Pete, and Adult Education

꧁

Dr. Bobby B. Dees was employed by the Alabama State Board of Education from September, 1974 through September, 1998. During his tenure he served as the Director of the Alabama Adult Education Program and Administrator of GED Testing. Remembering those years he said, "I met Pete in October 1974. I had been on the job with the Alabama State Department of Education for a month. A couple of people in the department introduced me to Pete and said, 'Bobby, we want you to meet Mr. Pete. He is a state legislator and he loves adult education.' So, we hit it off. That's been 45 years ago. Since then, up until two or three years ago, there has not been a week that Pete and I have not been together. He adopted me and I adopted him. He was just like a dad to me."

"Pete had three unmarried aunts who did not finish high school. Like most farm people they had to work, but they were educated in life, self-educated. He has told that story many, many times, to the legislature and to others. We had him speaking at engagements throughout the state constantly. He always spoke at our annual function. He was our safety-net person in the legislature. He was known in the legislature as the Father of Education. Any questions that came up about education, from the governor on down, whoever needed to know didn't go researching, they would just ask Pete, on the floor, privately, wherever. They sought his advice. We depended on him for our funding because some superintendents, from time to time, would cut out a department's line item if it was not their pet program. If you became THE omitted line item you didn't have a budget, therefore, you didn't have a program.

Pete watched it. He literally, many times, would contact adult education personnel to get the word out that our budget had been cut or had been totally marked out, Xed, within the last 8 or 10 hours before the vote to approve it. So, we had a network with our local coordinators and key legislators, able to contact them any time it was needed. We never lost funding, thanks to Pete, and he saw to it that we usually had additional funding. It wasn't just for adult education. It was for all education. Education was his love and joy, K-12 through post secondary, higher education, adult education, all of education. We depended on him. Without him we could not have operated."

"Pete was instrumental in helping our professional association, the Alabama Association for Public Continuing Adult Education, when it was formed about 45 years ago. As President of ALAPCAE, I introduced the idea of scholarships being given in Pete's name because he was the strongest advocate ever in the state legislature for adult education and educational programs at all levels. We in adult education were consistently recognized nationally for quality service provided and for large numbers of participants in literacy classes, ESL (English as a Second Language), GED (General Education Development) recipients, basic education for the homeless and the incarcerated, and for workforce development. We could not have been successful in delivering those quality and diverse services had it not been for that "sparkplug" in the legislature, Pete Turnham. We were averaging over 10,000 high school dropouts each year who were going through our programs and earning their high school equivalency, GED." There are nine annual Pete B. Turnham scholarships given each year by the ALAPCAE for two-year colleges. A $500 scholarship is available for one GED graduate from each of ALAPCAE's nine board districts to pay for tuition and/or books at a college of the student's choice.

"I also nominated Pete, and got the electorate to endorse it, for the American Association for Adult and Continuing Education President's Award." (Formed in 1926 as the American Association for Adult Education, and, via several mergers until 1982, it became the American Association for Adult and Continuing Education). "One award per year is given to the person who legislatively and otherwise is the strongest advocate for adult education. Pete received the award, presented in Las Vegas, and he and Alabama got a great deal of national attention. Up until then, Pete was the only person from the state of Alabama who had ever received the award."

"During those years Dr. Jo Smith was coordinator of the adult education program in the community junior college in Selma. She had the idea that if she could buy a little teaching lab, or if someone would donate a small trailer, she could drive it every day, park it in the rural areas where people many times would not admit they did not finish high school, and they could go there to work on their GED, enabling them to get a job. Another program we started was with human resources. We got 75 to 100 ladies each year who could barely read and write. They earned their GEDs, which they wanted so they could discontinue public assistance. Pete helped start these programs."

"We also started programs in the prison system. With Pete's help, we instigated a move to teach in the prisons. Every prison in the state of Alabama, where our program was, would allow us to screen the prisoners to make sure we got the people who needed and wanted to be there so that when they got out they were able to get a job. Most did not have skills, not even knowing how to fill out an application. We taught them how to look for a job, how to present themselves for a job, what type questions would be asked to see what their skills were, and then we taught them how to fill out an application."

"Pete is the kind of person who is magnetic. Like Pete, I love people in all walks of life. Whether you can read or write makes no difference to me. I like you for who you are. So, Pete and I just hit it off and bonded. Throughout my whole working career Pete was extremely involved and a strong advocate for our program. I recall we had a state superintendent who didn't want his staff members to become friends with the legislators. He even tried to pass a state rule that nobody could go to the capital and meet with any legislator at any time for any reason, even if a formal request was made. If they were seen there it was grounds for insubordination. The ink on that letter did not get dry before Pete got it. He sat down with the man and said it would not work and that he knew he (Pete) would be involved in all aspects of education. He said adult education was his pet project and he was going to be meeting with Bobby Dees. That's how strongly Pete felt about adult education. He said, 'How can I get on the floor and advocate a need for funds? For example, in my last conversation with Bobby, I asked how much money they needed as an increase. We're looking at

BOBBY DEES

113

all the budget line items. As to your financial needs and project results, what do you need?' We calculated the numbers, because at that time approximately one out of every three adults 21 years or older was a high school drop out. We knew if we could buy just one workbook per person the total cost would be over a million dollars. I knew we were not going to get that much in one year, so, we watered it down a little bit. Then we would have the facts, along with the realistic expectation, to ask for and receive the funds. The people who make the decisions for funding don't always know the needs. But, because Pete was helping us, they didn't question our budget request. We didn't get more money every year, but we never lost money. Other programs did lose money. So, we moved from a part time position at the local level, getting enough money to network with the two year and four year schools, to having a full time coordinator to run the program for several counties. I met with the school superintendents, got Pete involved, and said, 'All of you are competing for public publicity about your programs, and advertising the age brackets and numbers who have never finished school. If you would each take the $10,000 you are appropriated, pool it together, and manage it yourselves, you could hire a full time coordinator to network with business and industry to provide educational and job training to the people on the job.' For example, a paint company had one person who could not read very well, put just a fraction too much of one color in a paint, and it cost the company a lot of money. We would go into a company like that and assess the level of the employees' skills. We would start them at whatever level they were, and we taught them in compliance with and in line with what their job required. We would take their manuals, and some could not even read them, and build their instructional program around them. Another example is the catfish industry, the 1st or 2nd largest industry in Alabama. The average requirement in that industry decades ago was a low elementary grade level performance. We would go to the company, share what we could do, and partner with them. Then, they would fund the teacher because we did not have the funds. It was those kinds of programs for which Pete would help get the funds, to help the undereducated people with jobs."

"Pete is such a giver. There was not a month that Pete did not call me before the sun came up to tell me of someone who, maybe because of a fire, lost their house during the night, lost everything. He would say he needed me to call the volunteer groups I was involved with and tell them we needed donations, clothes, anything. Then he would check back with me the next morning and he'd meet me somewhere to get whatever I had collected. If he knew somebody didn't have food he would take produce from his garden and lay it at their door. I'm a strong advocate for helping people, and a lot of that influence came from Pete. Pete is always uplifting and never complains."

"I'm from Franklin, Alabama. Pete knows all my family and he's been to my family reunions. When my folks would get sick and die, Pete was there. I have always said there is nobody on the planet who has been to as many funerals as Pete has. He has an outstanding ability to know people and to call them by name. He is loved by so many."

Honored As He Works

$\sim\!\!\text{\textsection}\!\!\text{\textsection}\!\!\text{\textsection}\!\!\text{\textcopyright}$

DEDICATION OF
GILMER-TURNHAM BUILDING
LEFT TO RIGHT - AUDREY WATKINS
(PETE'S GRANDDAUGHTER), PETE,
MRS. M. D. GILMER, AND EMILY KEYS
(MRS. GILMER'S GRANDDAUGHTER)

After giving so much time and effort to help those with special needs, in 1976 Pete was the recipient of the Layman Award from the Alabama Rehabilitation Association.

In May of 1978 a very special event occurred in Pete's life and the life of Auburn University. Pete and Mrs. M.D (Pete) Gilmer were present for the dedication of the Gilmer-Turnham Diagnostic and Chemical Laboratories Building on Wire Road. Pete's granddaughter, Audrey Watkins, and Mrs. Gilmer's granddaughter, Emily Keys, cut the ceremonial ribbon marking the opening of the new building. The Diagnostic and Chemical Lab facilities are used to check feed, fertilizer, pesticides, and lime products for farmers, with testing facilities being

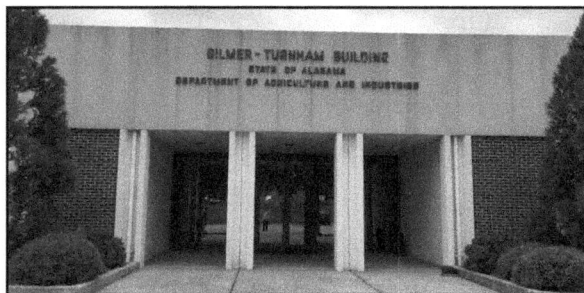

used for livestock and poultry protection for farmers around the state. The building was named for Pete and Mr. Gilmer because they had worked together on the funding and planning of the project, seeing it come to reality at a cost of $1.7 million. Mr. Gilmer, who died in 1976, was the former com-

117

missioner of Agriculture and Industries and was an employee of that organization for more than 40 years.

Another special moment for Pete, along with Ted Little, was presenting Auburn University Athletic Director Lee Hayley a copy of the joint Senate-House resolution honoring Auburn's SEC All Sports Championship in 1977-78. The resolution was sponsored by Pete and Ted and signed by Gov. George Wallace.

At the June 1979 graduation ceremony at Southern Union State Junior College in Wadley, Pete, as head of the House Education Committee and as the commencement speaker, told the graduates that they "would not find any state which offers more than Al-

PORTRAIT IN LOBBY OF
GILMER-TURNHAM BUILDING

abama." He challenged them "to live as your teachers and friends have taught you and to participate in your church, state, and nation, never forgetting your importance as an individual and the importance of the world around you." In commenting on educational legislation during his address he stated he was one of the original sponsors of the bill setting up the junior college system and that he was "working to see that you don't lose support of your off-campus operations. I want to make it clear that the Legislature alone can determine your destiny. No one can tear down the good work of junior colleges unless the Legislature approves."

Pete co-sponsored Act 79-348, which passed in July, and stated, "Relating to Chambers County: to authorize the county commission to impose a privilege or license tax upon the sale, use, or consumption of malt or brewed beverages; to provide for the administration and enforcement of this act; and to provide for the rate and distribution of the proceeds of the tax." The tax was four cents on each twelve ounces or fractional part thereof on any malt or brewed beverage sold within the county. Fifty percent was prorated among all city and county boards of education for educational purposes, and fifty percent was to be prorated among the Chambers County Commission general fund and the municipalities within the county.

In September, groundbreaking ceremonies were held in the Southeast corner of Auburn's new industrial park for the family-owned and operated Leonard Paterson Co., Inc., which moved to Auburn from Chicago. The firm had been making laboratory furniture and equipment since 1890, and Pete had laid the groundwork for the relocation of the plant, bringing new jobs to the people of Lee County.

In 1980 Pete sponsored the bill that made the wild turkey Alabama's state game bird. In a somewhat-less-than-serious debate over whether the wild turkey should be named to such a prominent state, Pete praised the wily bird, saying, "He's cagey and smart, like most Alabamians. He's humble, he's hard to get to, and he's smarter than some Alabamians I know." When asked if making the wild turkey the state game bird would mean the flicker, or yellow-hammer, would no longer be the state bird, Pete said it was two separate categories. Then said, "The turkey is a bird that can stand up for Alabama. If the yellow-hammer stood up for Alabama, you wouldn't know it!"

ALABAMA'S FAVORITE, Montgomery—The Alabama House has voted to make the wild turkey Alabama's state game bird. Rep. Pete Turnham of Auburn, sponsor of the bill, shows what a fine specimen Alabama grows. He brought the stuffed turkey to the state Capitol.

AUGUST 1981 - KAY RECEIVES HER SECOND MASTER'S DEGREE LEFT TO RIGHT - AUDREY WATKINS (GRANDDAUGHTER), DIANE, JOE, KAY, RUTH RICE (MOTHER), PETE, TIM, AND RUTHMARY

In August 1981 there was another proud event for the Turnham family when Kay received her second Master's degree from Auburn from the School of Education. After running her own private kindergarten for many years, Kay finished her career teaching in public school.

In 1981 Pete received the Patriotic Award from the VFW Post 5404 Ladies Auxiliary. Also, in that year he was a member of the Alabama State Department of Education's Community Education Advisory Council and was responsible for getting a resolution passed by the legislature honoring community education.

Speaking at the fall meeting of the Russell County Association for Mental Health, Pete predicted that the East Alabama area was close to getting a mental health center to serve a multi-county area, including Russell and Lee. He said it would be located in Opelika, "close to the center of masses of people", and would mean that the mentally ill could receive treatment closer to home without going to Bryce, Partlow, or Searcy Hospitals. "We will be able to treat about 85 percent in the county from which they come".

In 1981 Pete again ran for re-election to the Alabama State House of Representatives, and won his 6th term, to begin in 1982, becoming the top-ranking member, with 24 years of service. Some of the many reasons his constituency supported him was his recent honor of being presented the Outstanding Service Award in Alabama for his work in Community and Adult Basic Education, his sponsoring of Act 310 which established Community Mental Health Centers all over Alabama, his ability to push through legislation that started the kindergarten programs, and getting legislation passed that established Rural Resources Development programs in Alabama.

Notes from another of Pete's speeches…

Listen to this story of a man who failed.

1. *3 years of formal education*
2. *Failed in business at 31*
3. *Defeated for legislature at 32*
4. *Failed again in business at 33*
5. *Elected to Legislature at 34*
6. *Defeated for Congress at 43*
7. *Elected to Congress at 46*
8. *Defeated for Congress at 48*
9. *Defeated for Senate at 55*
10. *Defeated for Senate at 56*

This man happened to be none other than Abe Lincoln.

In meeting the challenge of the hour keep in mind:

    a. One step won't take you very far – You've got to keep on walking.

    b. One word won't tell folks who you are – You've got to keep on talking.

    c. One deed won't nearly do it all – You've got to keep on going.

    d. One inch won't make you very tall – You've got to keep on growing.

You will soon learn that:

1. *Freedom is not free – it must be earned and re-earned by each generation. Five major wars lasting through 26 years of our 180 year history - 1½ million men paid their last full measure from Bunker Hill in 1775 to Korea in 1953.*

2. *Unless you stand for something you will fall for almost anything.*

3. *It is dangerous to know the price of everything and the value of nothing.*

I wish I could predict your future, but you could be scared to death – You will probably be told that:

1. *Things won't change*

2. *You will make the same mistakes other generations have made*

   a. *A man named Ted Williams stepped to bat in Boston a few years ago to play his last game before finishing a long 19 year baseball career*

   b. *Babe Ruth struck out 1300 times*

   c. *Don't worry about mistakes – 30 million people take sleeping pills because of worry –*

Hit a homerun! You must be different!

WORK

1. *Few people ever failed in life who worked*

2. *Work is one of life's most rewarding blessings*

3. *Success is 90% work, 10% brains*

4. *Yet, there are some people who dislike all forms of work – They are sick – They need treatment –*

5. *True happiness comes from work, for in our work we see come forth:*

   a. *Confidence in ourselves and our society*

   b. *Self-reliance*

   c. *Accomplishment - all from being needed – from serving, working and giving-*

Mr. Pete

True nobility is being superior to your previous self.

STUDY – EDUCATION

Civilization has suddenly become a race between education and catastrophe. There is a shortage of 135,000 teachers in the USA. The upper ¼ won't go to college – College graduates make $200,000 a year more – Study prepares you to serve –

In Alabama there are:

830,000 pupils in public schools

28,000 teachers

30,000 in college

10,000 in mental hospitals

140,000 on welfare

Steve and Pete
Side by Side

Steve Flowers, a Troy native, was elected State Representative from Pike County and began serving in 1982. He had been a page in the Alabama Legislature at age 12 and worked at the Capital throughout high school, continuing his political interests by attending the University of Alabama and majoring in political science and history. When he was elected to the legislature at the age of 30, he received the largest number of votes ever received by any political candidate in Pike County history.

Steve said, "When I started in the legislature Pete sort of selected me. They do give deference for seating on the floor of the House. As a freshman, I would have been relegated to the back row. I don't know if Pete remembered me when I was a page or what it was, but Pete took me under his wing. Maybe he was in charge of the seating arrangement, but the next thing I knew I was off the back row and was seated by Pete Turnham, Pete's seat-mate. The only thing we had in common was that we were the only representatives from college towns. I had Troy and Pete had Auburn, and, other than that, I don't know why Pete chose me. I was very honored. Mr. Pete was a legend. He saw and made a lot of history. People would ask how I got up front as a freshman and I would say, 'Mr. Pete Turnham had me sit by him.' It was a grand seat, up front and center. Pete had already been there longer than anybody else and he was considered the Dean of the House. If the Speaker recognized him he would say, 'I recognize the gentleman from Lee, Dean of the House, Mr. Pete Turnham.' "

"Pete and I both commuted. Auburn had that straight interstate and it was less than an hour to Montgomery and I was from Troy and would drive down 231, so

123

we didn't have to spend the night, which made it a lot easier than for those who did have to spend the night. There were three of us that sat together, Jack Venable from Tallassee, a Representative for Elmore County, Pete from Auburn, and me from Troy. Jack owned the Tallassee Tribune and would go home to put it to bed every Thursday, Pete would go home to his garden, and I'd go home to Troy. We were all three buddies."

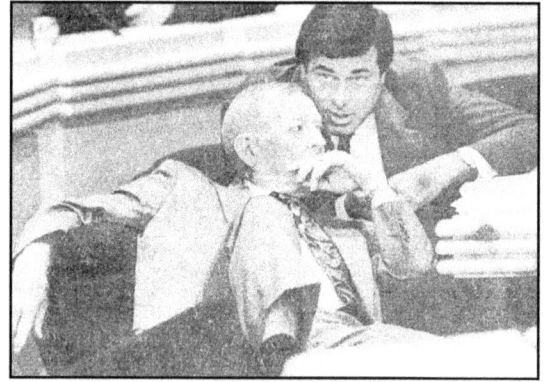

PETE AND STEVE CONFERRING

"Pete's generation was, indeed, the greatest generation. Pete epitomizes the Tom Brokaw book, The Greatest Generation. Pete also epitomizes this philosophical tenet. Even though they were conservative, men who came out of that depression era were progressive. They were FDR Democrats. Coming out of the depression, for about a 15 or 20-year window after the war, the south was somewhat void of the racial politics to come because African Americans didn't vote. It was a Jim Crow society so it wasn't an issue. African Americans were relegated to being second-class citizens without any voting rights so there would be no reason to slur them or race bait. Politicians in some of the southern states would get on the Senate floor and make racist speeches, but our Alabama senators then, Lister Hill and John Sparkman, were very erudite gentlemen and they wouldn't do that. They were in Washington to make sure Alabama got its part of the New Deal. Pete had that same philosophy. I never saw Pete vote against a tax and it never hurt him politically. I'd say, 'Pete, why are you voting for that tax?' and he would say, 'We've got to help the school children.' Those men were brought up in that New Deal. You wouldn't call them liberals. Everybody in the South loved FDR. Everybody in the country did. Alabama and the South were the pit of the country. No industrialization. So, the New Deal transformed the Tennessee Valley in the state of Alabama. So many people didn't even have indoor plumbing. Pete saw that. People who had seen the depression knew the value of a dollar, but they also felt like government should be part of the solution. People in the next generation sort of had a Republican philosophy of laissez faire – Ya'll look after yourselves. The government shouldn't be doing this. Let's have low taxes and less government. Pete's answer was always, 'I've got to help take care of the old folks and school children.' He really wanted to help people. If someone came to him with a problem he would try to help them with it. If a farmer came in and said he was having a problem, Pete would look into it and try to help him. That's why he never got beat. He had a tough race one time when the other most powerful person in Lee County, Bo Torbert, ran against him. Bo Torbert was very powerful in Lee County, but Pete beat him.

PETE AND STEVE FLOWERS

"Pete is very humble. He wouldn't toot his own horn. I never heard Pete say a cross word or a profane word, and I never heard him say a negative word about anybody. He was a gentleman. There would be those who would be dilatory and acrimonious toward those of us who would be considered conservative or pro-business, but Pete didn't take it personally. He was always upbeat. I never saw him in a bad mood. I sat by him for 16 years and I never saw him lose his temper. He has a lot of class, a real gentleman. And I never heard anybody say anything bad about him. He was always sort of happy, too. He was optimistic. Pete loves his family, his garden, and Auburn University, and I'm not sure in what order!"

"When Pete first started in the Legislature politicians and legislators had a lot of power. They could get people jobs with the state, and they could do more then than they can now. There was no merit system, so all state employees got their jobs through legislators. Pete came from that era and he would try to help everybody."

My daughters loved Pete. They were pages when they were little girls and Pete watched them grow up. He would take us out to lunch sometime at the Capital City Club and my daughters loved going there in Pete's big car."

"In the later years, before the parties changed, we were either in pro-business or a pro-trial lawyer group. We had this tort issue. Those of us who were in the business group, which would be Republicans today, mostly were conservative Democrats. Pete and I were in that group. It had already become somewhat of a philosophical rift that in his first years were more harmonious. It was not a partisan divide but a philosophical divide. Out of 105 House members I would say that 70 of us were in the pro business group and 35 were in the pro labor, pro AEA, and pro trial lawyer group. Out of our 70, 60 of us ran as Democrats. Through all this Pete's main mission was to not let those political wars hurt Auburn and to make sure Auburn got its fair share of the appropriations. He knew how things worked and where the money was, so he did his work in the committee meetings. Mr. Pete's personal mission was to look out for Auburn University. I watched him year after year get additional appropriations placed into Auburn's budget. He served on the Ways and Means Committee and knew where money was hidden in the budget. Because of Mr. Pete, Auburn got its fair share. I dare say that no man in history has meant more to Auburn."

During the 16 years I sat with Pete, I bet there were at least a dozen people who would come up and hug his neck. He and Kay had basically adopted them and let them come to their house when they were in Auburn. It must have been an experience like they were at home. I saw that happen, and it's probably a conservative number, at least a dozen times. We'd be walking down the hall and some person would hug his neck like he was their uncle. I would say, 'Mr. Pete, those people love you. Why do they like you so much?' and he would say, 'Kay and I adopted them while they were at Auburn.' He looked after them while they were there. "

"You build lasting friendships when you sit beside someone for that long a time. Pete helped people whether they helped him or not. That was just Mr. Pete. I truly love him. He has a lot of class, a real gentleman."

Moving Ahead and
More Rewards

*I*n January 1983 Pete received the Award of Merit at the National Association for Public Continuing Adult Education Annual International Convention in San Antonio, Texas for his efforts to promote adult education. The organization honors annually the person outside the field of adult education who has contributed the most to adult education. Pete was cited especially for his legislative efforts to bring about adult education teachers receiving the same raise as all other teachers. He also testified before the National Council on Adult Education concerning the revision of the Federal Adult Education Act.

On April 15, 1983, Pete lost his dad, "Mr. Henry", at the age of 92. He had been a proud supporter and companion of Pete through the years, often attending one of Pete's talks when the event was in or close to Abanda.

In 1984 Dr. James E. Martin became the new president of Auburn University. Both graduates of the Auburn School of Agriculture, he and Pete worked closely together to determine and secure funds for their alma mater.

That same year, the Turnham-Goodwin Act was passed, providing the money for the building of the new long awaited Lee County Health Department, to be financed through a $45-million-dollar Public Health Facilities Bond Issue, which would be paid for with about $4 million a year produced by increased hazardous wastes taxes at the hazardous waste facility in Emelle, in Sumter County. Pete piloted the bill through the House and Sen. Earl Goodwin piloted it through the Senate. Pete said he began working on the act in October of 1983, traveling around talking to legislators and "observing poor facilities in such poor condition." He said a new building "would give them more room to operate, help staff be more efficient, and with new methods of treatment, it will be built to accommodate new machinery, and more parking."

Ever mindful of the needs of the School of Agriculture at Auburn University, Pete received the following letter in May 1984, after securing funds for the poultry department.

> *Dear Pete,*
>
> *At times we take lightly the support you give Auburn University and its varied programs. I can assure you that the faculty of this department recognizes and values your judgment. You were not supportive of the poultry industry's recent efforts on behalf of our research and teaching programs because of votes in your district, but rather, because of your judgment that poultry is an important segment of Alabama agriculture.*
>
> *The faculty in this department will be ever grateful for your efforts and will prove your judgment correct.*
>
> *You must set a time to visit our research unit and make arrangements to get some "farm-fresh eggs".*
>
> *Sincerely,*
> *Claude H. Moore,*
> *Head Poultry Science*

Also in 1984, Pete co-sponsored an act raising the salaries for Lee County probate judge, sheriff, tax assessor, and tax collector.

In January 1985, Pete co-sponsored an act to insure that "no child care or day care center, nor child care institution or institution for child care, in Lee County, shall be allowed to operate on a twenty-four-hour basis unless the department of pensions and security shall first approve of such operation."

In February, Pete, who served on the board of directors of the Southeast Alabama Sickle Cell Association, along with State Senator Ted Little, promoted and supported state funding for the Southeast Alabama Sickle Cell Association and Clinic for free testing for sickle cell anemia, hypertension, and other general health care tests in the Opelika school system, as well as making home visits to sickle cell victims in Lee and the surrounding counties.

The Rice-Turnham act in 1986 authorized the county commission in Lee County to establish fire districts and to provide fire fighting and fire prevention services for dwellings, commercial structures, field and forest lands through the use of volunteer fire departments in cooperation with the Alabama Forestry Commission.

In June Pete, touted as "Mr. Education" in the Alabama Legislature, delivered the commencement speech at Southern Union State Junior College in Wadley.

Another election in November prompted this "special message" from Pete in the newspapers.

"I am a lifelong Democrat because the Democratic Party is the party of the working men and women of this country. I choose the party and I have served longer in the Alabama House of Representatives than any other member – always as a Democrat working for the best interests of the people of this area and all the people of the state.

During the last primary, I received a vote of confidence from more than 40,000 voters. I am humbled by that expression of support and confidence. I will be on the ballot next Tuesday – along with some of the state's most outstanding political leaders – all Democrats.

They care about Alabama and East Alabama, in particular. Leading our ticket are Bill Nichols, Bill Baxley, Richard Shelby, John Rice and Dutch Higginbotham. I will appreciate your vote for me and just as much I will appreciate your votes for those who will lead our party as we tackle some of the most pressing problems now facing our state.

I urge you to cast an informed ballot, a ballot for experienced, capable, dedicated and honorable leadership."

Elected again, Pete began his 7th term as a State Representative in the Alabama House of Representatives.

Nominated by his peers for his distinguished public service, Pete was presented the Award of Merit as the Outstanding Legislator for 1986.

In 1987, Pete was awarded the "Legislator of the Year Award" by the Alabama Nurses Association at their 74th annual conference in Tuscaloosa "In honor and with deep appreciation of the distinguished service rendered promoting

TURNHAM WINS NURSING AWARD — Alabama Representative Pete Turnham of Auburn recently was awarded the "Legislator of the Year Award" by the Alabama Nurses Association. The award was given to Turnham for his work in support of legislation involving a third party reimbursement plan for nurses.—AU Photo issues and programs that encourage quality health care" particularly for his work in support of legislation involving a third party reimbursement plan for nurses.

As the compassionate person Pete is, he was recognized as a strong supporter of adequate funding for the Alabama Institute for Deaf and Blind, and he presided at the 1987-88 budget presentation and hearing in Montgomery for the funds for the organization, allocated by the House. He also co-sponsored an Act to authorize the Lee County Board of Health to annually fix a schedule of fees for services rendered pursuant to the duties with which the board was charged, and to provide for the annual examination of documented indigent residents free of charge.

In 1988, Pete co-sponsored the Act to levy a 2% lodging tax to establish the Alabama-Opelika Convention and Visitors Bureau, and he headed sponsorship of the Act which provided that any member of the teachers' or employees' retirement system of Alabama could use accumulated sick leave toward time required for retirement. Previously, Pete had sponsored a bill to relieve certain school superintendents of threatened liability in granting teachers sick leave. It had been the custom for teachers to accumulate one day a month, or nine days of sick leave during the school year, and they could use up to 45 days in five years, in any one year after the accumulation. An attorney general opined that, under the law, teachers could only take a maximum of 20 days in a year. As a consequence, state examiners auditing the books of a number of county school boards were threatening to charge back to the superintendents for the time teachers took in excess of 20 days. Pete's bill was to correct the difficulty and restore the original plan, permitting teachers to use all 45 days of sick leave, if necessary, in one year.

In November, Pete received a Certificate of Appreciation from the East Alabama Regional Planning and Development Commission and East Alabama Child Development Program on behalf of the children and families served "In grateful acknowledgement of your continued support of children and families; in recognition of your significant contribution in securing funding; and in tribute to your advocacy of quality child care for the children of Alabama." In December he received the Distinguished Service Award "In sincere appreciation of Community Involvement by the Alabama-West Florida Civitan District."

Pete enjoyed speaking in his own church as well as others and the following are notes he made for a Christmas talk:

SUNDAY

1. *Holly and other green decorations date back to pagan times. Why use green? Why kiss under mistletoe? Why hang wreaths? Why is ivy seldom used inside? Why is mistletoe never used in a church? What was the first plant ever used in Xmas decoration? Some true, some fanciful, some still causing man to wonder at the miracle of enduring life in the midst of winter death.*

2. *Primitive forefathers used green branches in magical rites to ensure return of vegetation to earth. To early converts it was natural to use greens as a symbol of the Christ Child's birth. Church first opposed this, but later accepted this pagan custom in Christian service. Some plants of long ago are still in use today. Others have fallen by the way.*

3. *HOLLY – green leaves, red berries, a natural for Christmas decorations. To early Christians in Northern Europe this was a symbol of the burning bush of Moses and the flaming love for God that filled Mary's heart. Prickly points and red berries, resembling drops of blood, also reminded Christians that this child of Bethlehem was born to wear a crown of thorns. In Medieval England, holly was thought to have a special power against witchcraft. It kept young girls from turning into witches. Some say holly is a form of the word holy, and sprang up beneath footsteps of Christ as He first trod the earth.*

4. *IVY – In pagan Rome, ivy was the badge of the wine god, and was displayed as a symbol of unrestrained drinking and feasting. For this reason it was later banished from Christian homes in England and could only grow outside.*

5. *LAUREL – Emblem of triumph and victory. Used in many lands as decoration at Christmas to proclaim victory over sin and death, which Christ's birth signified. Used very little in America. Today's wreaths come from old Roman customs of hanging laurel wreath as a friendly greeting.*

6. *MISTLETOE – Held sacred by Druids and Norsemen, because it slew Balder, the sun god. Called the "golden bough", it is not acceptable for church decorations, even now. Thought to have miraculous powers. Kissing under it and giving berries… Bishops in England won't let it be used.*

7. *GLASTONBURY THORN TREE – Legend has it that after Christ's death, Joseph of Arimathea journeyed to England and settled at Glastonbury. He stuck his staff in the ground and it immediately took root and each*

Christmas produced white flowers. Joseph erected a chapel and this thorn became rallying point for all defenders of faith. In 1900, owner of this abbey gave a cutting to the first bishop in Washington.

8. <u>POINSETTIA</u> – *Not a flower but a bract of leaves.*
Named for Dr. Joel Poinsett, U.S. Ambassador to Mexico. 100 years ago, he brought this flower to his S.C. home where it now is used as a Christmas flower.

Can You Keep Christmas?

Are you willing to stoop down and consider the needs and the desires of little children; to remember the weakness and loneliness of people who are growing old; to stop asking how much your friends love you and to ask yourself whether you love them enough; to bear in mind the things that other people have to bear on their hearts; to trim your lamp so that it will give more light and less smoke, and to carry it in front so that your shadow will fall behind you; to make a grave for your ugly thoughts, and a garden for your kindly feelings, with the gate open – are you willing to do these things even for a day? Then you can keep Christmas! (no identification of author in the notes).

A CHRISTMAS GREETING
By Fra Giovanni – 1513 A.D.

I am your friend, and my love for you goes deep.
There is nothing I can give you which you have not got;
But there is much, very much, that, while I cannot give it
You can take.

No heaven can come to us unless our hearts
Find rest in today.
No peace lies in the future which is not hidden
In this present little instant.

The gloom of the world is but a shadow.
Behind it, yet within our reach, is joy.
There is radiance and glory in the darkness,
Could we but see, and to see, we have only to look.
I beseech you to look.

Life is so generous a giver, but we,
Judging its gifts by their covering,

Cast them away as ugly, or heavy, or hard.
Remove the covering, and you will find beneath it
a living splendor, woven of love, by wisdom, with power.

Welcome it, grasp it, and you touch the angel's hand
That brings it to you.
Everything we call a trial, a sorrow, or a duty,
Believe me, that angel's hand is there; the gift is there,
and the wonder of an overshadowing Presence.

Our joys too; be not content with them as joys.
They, too, conceal diviner gifts.
Life is so full of meaning and purpose,
So full of beauty - beneath its covering -
That you will find earth but cloaks your heaven.

Courage then to claim it: that is all!
But courage you have; and the knowledge that we
Are pilgrims together,
Wending through unknown country, home.

And so, at this Christmas, I greet you.
Not quite as the world sends greetings,
But with profound esteem and with the prayer
That for you now and forever,
The day breaks, and the shadows flee away.

As the Roman officer said — Surely, this man is the Son of God!

Always anxious to help his hometown, Pete welcomed Gov. Guy Hunt and his wife, Helen, to a covered dish supper, sponsored by the Abanda Volunteer Fire Department at Abanda First Baptist Church on March 6, 1989. Also in 1989, Pete became a charter member of the Alabama Rural Fire Caucus.

In May, a bill, co-sponsored by Pete became law, to provide that the legislature would have the power to provide that elected superintendents of education would be eligible to participate in the Teachers' Retirement System of Alabama as the legislature saw fit. And another Act was passed to create and establish a special abandoned mine land reclamation trust fund to receive and retain up to 10% of the appropriated funds granted annually to the U.S. Department of Interior for the reclamation of abandoned mine lands in Alabama.

In the fall of 1989, Pete began his 8th campaign to represent his constituency in the state House of Representatives, and he was voted in for his 8th term, to begin in 1990. By this time he was a 32 year House veteran and senior-ranking member of the Alabama Legislature, Vice-Chairman of the powerful House Ways and Means Committee, had served as Chairman and Treasurer of the Southern States Energy Board, served as a member of the Education Commission of the States, and as a member of the state study committee on adult literacy, to name a few of his accomplishments. He had sponsored hundreds of Alabama's laws, resolutions and commendations over three decades in the House, sponsored the bill to create Alabama's Public Kindergarten Program, was the sponsor of bond issues to build physical plants in Alabama for K-12 and institutions of higher education, sponsored and passed the 1990 Turnham-Goodwin Bill to construct public health facilities in Alabama, created Alabama's community mental health system, was Alabama's leading advocate for adult literacy and vocational training, led the fight in 1989 to get Auburn University its largest appropriation (over $150 million) in its history, and had served under seven different Alabama governors. At home he had four children, four grandchildren, one great-grandchild, owned and ran a business, was a founder and charter member of Lakeview Baptist Church, a member and deacon of Parkway Baptist Church, and was an active member of several civic organizations.

Once again, beginning a new term, Pete sponsored a bill to help people by providing an additional cost-of-living increase to certain retirees and beneficiaries receiving a monthly benefit from the employees' retirement system of Alabama.

A seasoned Representative by this time, Pete had learned early in his political career, when some irate legislators had called him a communist, that he would accomplish nothing by getting mad. He said, "You've got to find a way to cooperate and sometimes to sacrifice. In politics, you can't live off grudges and insults that you get from time to time, or you'll go crazy. You just have to brush them aside and part the waters and look for a drier spot to walk. If you do that you can keep a positive attitude." He learned quickly to respect opponents of his bills. "Sometimes they did you a favor but you didn't realize it at the time," he said. Pete said being called a communist in the mid 1960s was the worst name-calling he endured as a legislator, but added he'd had some stares that were worse than that. "When I started to try to pass the kindergarten bill, they literally laughed me off the floor. The old saying was, 'We don't have enough money to support the grades we've got now and here you are trying to create more.'" He said legislators accused him of being a communist as sponsor of the kindergarten bill for trying to control the minds of young children. "I think that very thing is the reason Alabama has so many illiterates," Pete said. "We have a million people in the state that function at the fourth grade level or below and 251,000 that can't even read their name in print."

In 1990, Pete was awarded the Guardian of Small Business Award by the National Federation of Independent Businesses, the criteria including voting record, sponsorship of small business legislation, leadership role in activities relating to small business issues, and active participation in floor debates concerning legislation of critical importance to small business.

Not unusual for Pete, he was awarded a citation for perfect attendance during the 1990 session of the Alabama Legislature.

After serving 32 years in the legislature, the longest on record, Pete said, "You have to like it. You have to like people. And you really have to want to serve. If you didn't want to serve and help people, it would run you crazy." Citing that it was not always easy, he said, "You get fussed at a lot. People have a tendency to get down on you. Then somebody will come along and thank you for some little deed you've done, and all that is forgotten. It's just a matter of good things canceling out the bad." Having worked with seven governors and looking back, Pete said, "The political setup was different back then. The governors controlled all the committee appointments, all the chairmen, and, of course, all his cabinet. They ran the government. Whatever they said went. You either went along or tried to get your way, and (if you got your way) you were unpopular until you could find a way to get back in the good graces with them. I was too stubborn sometimes to get back." Pete said lawyers dominated the Legislature when he first went to Montgomery. Incumbent lawmakers made it tough on newcomers and new members rarely received significant committee appointments. "They gave me the third degree the first few times I got up on the floor on a bill. They were trying to teach me a lesson. You had to learn the hard way." Pete always felt the way a lawmaker conducts himself on the House floor, his integrity and honesty, determined his success in passing bills. Saying the success of a lawmaker should not be determined by the number of bills he introduces, he said, "If you get four of five bills passed in a session, besides local bills, you are lucky. The reason is everybody doesn't see it the same. They may not think it is the best. In politics, you can't live off grudges. If you live off grudges and insults that you get from time to time, you'll go crazy. You just have to brush them aside and keep a positive attitude."

147

Always watching out for education and eying a $100 million shortfall in the education budget for 1991-92, Pete, in a letter, asked Governor Guy Hunt to call a special session to deal with the issue. Pete said, "It's not politics for me. I have school people look me in the eye and say, 'We are hurting, Pete.' It's for the children. They have got to compete with the other 49 states and the rest of the world." Pete felt there would not be a negative reaction from the voters at the suggestion of a tax increase, saying, "I have voted for every tax increase for schools for 33 years, and I've been coming back for 33 years." In the letter Pete said, "changes in the economy from the time the budget was passed until the present time, caused by the Persian Gulf crisis, the corporate tax decline, and other economic conditions warrant the state to come forward with meaningful solutions. I will do all in my power to help find sources to correct the shortfall if you see fit to call us into session." Pete stated, "Every candidate that ran statewide ran on a platform of putting education first. The least we can do is go in and pass a stopgap measure and let it self destruct when the proration is over." Feeling the governor would respond favorably, Pete said a special session before the April 16 start of the Legislature's regular session would allow the state to go ahead and start collecting the revenue immediately. Approaching the time for teachers to sign their contracts for the next year, Pete said, "This is critical."

In 1991, Pete sponsored a bill, which became law, to establish a Preschool Special Education Program for children with disabilities, ages 3 through 5 years. All county and city local education agencies were required to provide free appropriate public education for all eligible children with disabilities, ages 3 through 5 years, inclusive, in accordance with the Individuals with Disabilities Education Act.

A Turnham co-sponsored Act passed that same year authorizing Lee County to levy a tax on each ton or cubic yard of rock or other substance quarried in the county to provide funds to be expended on the repair or maintenance of roads and bridges.

Highly supported by the state PTA, Pete sponsored another bill which imposed a temporary one-cent sales tax to help bail school systems out of financial crises caused by state imposed budget cuts. The House voted 33-60 to reject the plan and, as a result, Pete "won" the 1991 Shroud Award, given by House members to the lawmaker who sponsored the proposed law that was surest to die. During the debate, a letter to the editor from a Montgomery resident stated, *"Rep. Pete Turnham shows more interest in the welfare and future of our school children than the vast majority of our elected officials, including our governor. It is a shame that we don't have more leaders like Mr. Turnham."*

Pete was also presented the 1991 Alabama Retired State Employees' Association Senior Achievement Award.

The life of a legislator is not easy on families. Kay learned to not look forward to vacations or to dinner with Pete in a restaurant without interruptions. They had to be creative in order to communicate. A note left on the corner of the kitchen table was usually more effective than trying to catch each other on the telephone. Growing up, the children didn't know what it was like to not have their father rushing to Montgomery and sometimes spending nights in meetings. But, according to their son, Joe, it didn't hurt them. "I think he was real sensitive to the fact that he was gone a lot in his personal profession as well as his job in the legislature," Joe said. "I was the youngest child and I was born later in life when he was probably the busiest. But, I think he was really sensitive and always set aside one-on-one time with me, real quality time – throwing a baseball in the yard, or getting off on Saturday to take me fishing or to an Atlanta Braves baseball game. He always made time for me and I never felt like his life as a public servant ever distracted from duties as a father to me, and that's probably true for all the children." Pete is very proud of his children and said he felt he let them learn to be independent.

In December Pete was chosen Auburn's Best Unsung Hero in the Opelika-Auburn News poll. He was nominated by Glen Gulledge because "he's a good fellow. A lot of people don't know much about him, but he's been a state representative for this area longer than anyone". When told he had won, Pete said, "How about that. It's quite flattering and I appreciate it. I feel like far more people than I are more deserving, but I will accept it on behalf of the whole Auburn community. I'm proud to be an Auburn University graduate and a member of the Auburn community. It's a great place to live."

Scott's Saturdays with Pete

Scott Couch met Pete in 1992. "I was in school at Auburn and Joe was my fraternity advisor. I was looking for a job and asked him if he knew anybody who needed some help. He said, 'I sure do. My Daddy needs somebody to help him in his garden.'" Sitting with Pete, he said, "I came over that Saturday morning and had breakfast with you and Mrs. Kay, and it all started back then, on the patio by the pool."

"Saturdays were Scott and Pete days. We were either at the farmers supply store, taking care of the cabin at Lake Martin, or taking care of the cemeteries in Abanda or Lanett. Several times coming back from working on the lake house we would have to call Mrs. Kay and tell her to go buy Benedryl because we got into a hornets nest and were covered in stings." (As more grandchildren arrived, Pete and Kay purchased a place on Lake Martin where days were spent with family, and Pete passed along his love of fishing to the next generation.)

When the garden was in season, every Saturday Pete and Scott would fill sacks full of produce and take them all over town to people who needed them. "Pete has two fig trees on his property that are very productive. August was fig-picking season, and between that and the garden we were busy. We would usually pick figs for about three weeks and end up with several hundred pounds of them. In the early days, Mrs. Kay would make fig preserves, but you can only make so much of that, so we would deliver them to people around town so they could eat them fresh or make preserves. People would often bring us home-made bread or other goodies in return."

Once, when Kay was on a trip to Japan, Pete and Scott worked on the burn pile near the creek on the lower side of the house. Scott said it got to be the size of a small house. They were working in the front yard when they decided to sit on the front porch to 'sit down and blow,' a saying from Pete's childhood which meant to take a break, sit down, and drink a cold Coca Cola. Soon they began to hear sirens. Per Scott, "The first vehicle to approach was a fire truck, which passed out of our view, and I commented that there must have been an accident. Then we heard sirens squealing and could tell the truck was backing up. Following quickly were three more fire trucks. I looked around the corner, could see flames coming over the house, and thought 'We're going to be taken to jail.' The fire trucks were blocking the street. The fire chief whipped into the driveway, got out and said, 'Hey Mr. Pete. We just came by to give you a burning permit.' He walked up and gave him the permit and told him to have a good day. They turned all the trucks around and away they went."

Scott, a political science major from Arkansas, helped Pete with his campaigns. "In 1993, Shane, my best friend from Arkansas, came to visit me and ended up staying in Auburn. When the next election came around we walked the entire city of Opelika going door to door campaigning for Pete. One time I had an elderly lady ask me where Pete was from and I told her Abanda. She said, 'Oh, my. I will vote for anyone that was born and abandoned!' "

Pete and Kay sponsored the annual Sunday School Christmas Banquet for the Adult Sunday School Class at Parkway Baptist Church, of which they were members, around the middle of December at the local country club each year. Pete said, "The members could invite who they wanted to as long as they paid for it. We got the club to do it for about $15 (per person)." Pete and Scott would go to CAFFCO in Montgomery and get a truckload of poinsettias, deliver several of them to friends during the week, then go to the club and decorate with the rest of them. After the banquet they would take them to the church to decorate for the Christmas service. Per Scott, "Every year, for

about 25 years, Pete sent two poinsettias home (Arkansas) to my mom and grandmother. Every year!" And every Easter they would go to CAFFCO and get Easter lilies, give them to Pete's friends, and decorate the church with them. There is a wall at Pete's house now lined with Easter lilies that Pete and Scott planted through the years.

Scott particularly remembers a bill Pete sponsored and which passed in 1998. "When cell phones started being used a lot in about 1998 you couldn't dial 911 from your cell phone. Mr. Pete sponsored the bill to add 70 cents to a person's phone bill to add the 911 connection."

Friday nights are Good Ol Boy nights. For fifteen plus years Pete and Kay and Bill and Rudine Wilson would go out to eat at Good Ol Boys Restaurant each week. Scott said, "One week Pete and Kay would pick up the Wilsons and go eat and then go back to the Wilsons for dessert. The next week the Wilsons would pick up Pete and Kay. This went on for a long time until health issues made it difficult for them to make it out there. Nothing would stop Pete from having his Good Ol Boys, so his solution was to have the Wilsons come to his house and send me out to get everyone's food. The owners of Good Ol Boys go to Parkway Baptist and Friday night is a big social occasion for everyone. As I pick up Pete's food I have to give all of his regards and then remember everyone who is there so I can tell him about it. Thankfully, by this time, I know almost everyone and they know me. To this day, Pete still gets his Good Ol Boys every Friday night; grilled lemon pepper catfish, baked potato, and steamed veggies."

Through the years Scott has worked side by side with Pete, their partnership a mutual dedication. When Hurricane Opal hit Auburn in 1994, Pete lost most of the trees in his yard. Scott took his two-week vacation from the bank where he works and stayed with Pete and Kay to help clean up. Then he worked the next month, in the evenings after working his regular job each day, to help Tim clean up his property. As the years passed, Scott began to drive Pete and Kay to night meetings. "Every award service, dinner, Boy Scout meeting, Agriculture Commission meeting, reunions, etc., I was their driver. Though I would have preferred to sit in the back, Pete always

SCOTT COUCH

141

insisted I sit at the head table and he introduced me as his guest of honor." Scott has had four major back surgeries and Pete always drove him to Birmingham to the hospital, visited with him, and picked him up when it was time to come home. After Kay was no longer able to cook, Pete did the cooking and Scott washed the dishes. Today, Scott does the grocery shopping and runs errands for Pete and always picks up Friday night dinner at Good Ol Boys. Affectionately, Scott says, "As Mr. Pete tells it, we have been best friends for 27 years and have never had a cross word between us."

Always Pushing Forward

*n 1992, Pete worked tirelessly for education. At that time, Alabama was the only southern state that had not passed some measure of reform. The Senate voted down the reforms that the House had passed, which meant the school districts would receive exactly the same amount of money they had received the previous year. And, by not including inflationary or cost-of-living adjustments for 1992 the districts would actually be receiving less money. Pete said, "I'm just sick over it. We're really hamstrung. It's tough when you work an entire session on something and then see it go flat at the last minute. Alabama has missed out on an opportunity to improve the state's educational system." As usual, the legislators concerns were that they would be criticized for raising taxes.

In an article Pete wrote for the August 1992 "Alabama Farmers' and Consumers' Bulletin,' a portion of what he said was…

> *"Agriculture ain't what it used to be and it never was." The point is that looking back to some past situation can be misleading because we forget the bad, remember the good, and fail to profit by past failures and successes. We treasure the agriculture of the past because it was made up of largely self-sufficient family units that were self-sustaining and yet able to offer some products for sale to others. We tend to forget that many of the agricultural practices of the past really were not all that good. Hand labor and horsepower by horses and mules was very demanding on the tillers of the soil, and many of our tillage practices were detrimental to soils, water sources, the environment, and other natural resources.*

In contrast to using a vast majority of the populace to produce food and fiber, agricultural practices of today allow less than 2 percent of our population in the U.S. to produce food and fiber for our own use and yet allow from 25 to 50 percent of various commodities to be exported to other countries. This low labor and high technology agriculture of today is frequently criticized for displacing labor from the farm.

Labor, indeed, has been moved from agriculture and freed up for the production of goods and services that would never have been possible as long as 50 to 75 percent of the population was needed to just produce food. This freed labor source can now process food and fiber into innumerable products that were not envisioned even 25 years ago. From convenience foods to clothing and other numerous products, we can live better for less in the U.S.

Henry Ford was no fool. He recognized the labor force from our farms as not only becoming available, as farming became more efficient, but also recognized this labor pool as being most responsible in their new manufacturing jobs. He literally sought out 'the first wave of laborers leaving the farm.' Ford's concept was so well founded that his laborers (and laborers going into other new non-agricultural professions) were the best customers for his cars. Ford was, indeed, a wise man with the right idea at the right time. Yet, he would have been a failure if agriculture had not steadily become more efficient so that farm labor could be employed by Ford and other industrial factories.

Ironically, Henry Ford and other tractor manufacturers laid the groundwork to hire more farmers as they rolled out both the early version of farm tractors and later versions in the post WWII era that eliminated all horse and mule power and reduced dramatically the human labor necessary for farming. Today's farms have many characteristics that must be recognized and studied if we are serious about continuing to improve the lot of agriculture and farming in general.

— Agriculture is larger today than ever in the U.S...

— Agriculture is specialized and streamlined...

— Agriculture is high technology...

— Agriculture is diverse...

— Agriculture has done more through USDA, Land Grant Universities, and the practicing farmer to stop soil erosion, restore forests and grasslands, and ensure clean waterways than most any other segment of our industrialized society.

— Agriculture remains, despite many changes in its practice and out put, the domain of all citizens...

We in the Alabama Legislature have a special challenge and responsibility to keep all of agriculture alive and well. We must do this well, for Alabama's four million people and the world's five billion plus people are depending on us."

In early 1993 there was a plan in the legislature to give mostly black Alabama State and Alabama A & M universities a $40 million spending package if those schools would drop their appeals in an 11-year desegregation lawsuit. Pete saw the plan as an attack on Auburn University that would divert money from Auburn and other schools for research and outreach that would duplicate work already done by Auburn, so he fought it. Comments made about Pete by some of the legislators trying to get the bill passed were: "Pete's got connections you don't realize he's got until you're trying to beat him. He's smart. He's cunning. He's like an old, sly fox. Even though he and I have gotten in some very strong arguments, he's always come to me as a gentleman and said, 'John, you know I had to do what I had to do.' He's very adamant about issues dealing with agriculture and farming. He's adamant about boll weevil eradication. He bleeds Orange and Blue. He's their protector. I respect that. We have these turf battles in the Legislature." - Rep. John Rogers, D- Birmingham. "What's important to Pete Turnham is whatever he perceives to be important to Auburn. I think he lives, breathes, and acts Auburn. I find him a very likable person – very easy to talk to, very jovial, very even-tempered. It's very difficult to dislike Pete Turnham." – Rep. Demetrius Newton, D-Birmingham. "He is willing to fight guerrilla warfare on behalf of Auburn University. I would do the very same thing, and likely with not as much tenacity and skill, if Auburn were the core of my district." – Rep. Bill Fuller, D-LaFayette.

On August 30th, Kay and Pete were honored at their church with a beautiful 50th wedding anniversary recep-

KAY AND PETE'S 50TH WEDDING ANNIVERSARY

1943   1993
Pete and Kay
Turnham

tion celebrating their August 25, 1943, marriage, another testament to their love, devotion, and life partnership.

In a 1993 interview Pete answered questions about legislators from the time he took office in 1958 until the present. Asked if legislative service was attracting the quality of people it once did he answered, "No. It's not attracting the same sort of people it used to. I don't know quite how to say it, but it's different now. When I first came to the House it was almost a sacred thing to serve in the Legislature. It was an honor. It was a position of respect. It is not that way any more. I am not saying we don't have some fine legislators today. We do. We just seemed to have more of them in the past." Another question concerned the current proliferation and influence of lobbyists. Pete's response was, "I can name just about every lobbyist there was when I first came to the House. I don't think there was more than a dozen. Today there must be hundreds. I am not saying lobbyists are bad people. They're not. But so many of them have their PACs (Political Action Committee) and their money and the temptations are awful strong on folks who have never been exposed to this kind of thing before. We've got to put a limit on PAC campaign contributions. We need to outlaw the laundering of campaign money by transferring it from PAC to PAC, and we must make it absolutely clear that campaign funds cannot be converted to personal use." As a final thought, Pete said, "Don't forget that every legislator, the good and the bad, was elected by the people of his or her district. If folks are looking for somebody to blame about the quality of the Legislature, all they have to do is look in the mirror."

Another milestone for Pete was getting a tax credit for businesses that organized literacy training programs for their workers, stating it would be good for the companies, workers, and communities. Pete said effective workplace literacy programs "can result in the elimination of unemployment, the improvement of job skills, and the betterment of an industry because the people have been upgraded in their education to where they can work the machines." He estimated that if 1,000 businesses took part in the project at approximately $144 per worker, a 20 percent tax credit would cost the state about $288,000. But better trained and better educated workers would qualify for higher salaries, and higher salaries would mean more taxes paid, meaning the state would gain from the programs.

Having sponsored and seen the Act passed in 1991 to guarantee special education services to children with disabilities ages 3 through 5, and always trying to get help for those in need, especially by way of education, Pete sponsored an Act, which passed, to establish a program to provide early intervention services for infants and toddlers with disabilities and their families. The program included assistive technology devices and services; audiology; family training, counseling, and home visits; health services; medical services for diagnostic or evaluation purposes; nursing services; nutrition services; occupational therapy; physical therapy; psychological services; service coordination services; special work services; special instruction; speech-language pathology; vision services; and transportation and related costs necessary to enable the infant or toddler and family to receive the early intervention services.

In continuous demand as a speaker, in 1994 Pete spoke to many organizations, beginning the year as guest speaker at the Southside Baptist Church of Alabaster on Baptist Men's Day. Other events included the Auburn Lions Club, where he was presented a new watermelon variety called AU Sweet Scarlet, the Auburn Civitan Club, the Lee County Extension where he was honored for his support of family legislation, and the Alabama Association for Public Continuing Adult Education at their annual board meeting where he was presented a proclamation "for his active involvement in providing adult education services and educational opportunities for the last two decades. He is a leader in the field of adult education where he has been the recipient of the State of Alabama and the National Association for Public Continuing Education Annual Outstanding Contributors' award for the United States of America."

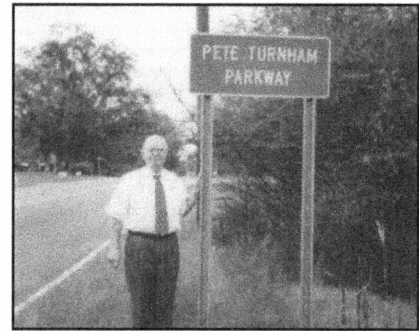

PETE HONORED WITH HIGH-
WAY THROUGH ABANDA,
NAMED FOR HIM

In March, Pete was honored when Highway 77 from La-Fayette to Wadley through his home community of Abanda was named for him. The section of road thenceforth became known as the Pete Turnham Parkway with signs along the highway denoting the honor.

On September 30, 1994, as a 50-year alumnus of Auburn University, Pete proudly became a "Golden Eagle." Be-

147

cause of his status as an outstanding graduate he was honored by being asked to give the class welcome.

In the fall of 1994, Pete campaigned for his 10th term in the Alabama House of Representatives. With 36 years of experience he retained his seat and began his 37th year of service.

On December 14, 1819, after Congress passed the resolution of admission, President James Monroe signed the document making Alabama a state. 175 years later Pete celebrated with the 500 children at Wright's Mill Road School in Auburn by cutting a cake which was in the shape of Alabama, and singing with the students the state song and Happy Birthday to Alabama. Pete presented the school with a new state flag and reminded the first through fourth graders to take care of the state's natural resources. "Alabama has 10 percent of the nation's iron ore, coal, water, and atomic power," he said. "We need to take care of our resources. Our job is to make it better." In conclusion, he said, "This is a beautiful celebration. These kids will remember this forever."

The year ended in a most fitting way when Pete, his tireless support and love of his alma mater acknowledged, was recognized by the Auburn University Board of Trustees for a 'life well lived' and presented with the 130th Auburn University honorary doctor of laws degree at the winter commencement service on December 9, 1994. About the honor Auburn President William V. Muse said, "Mr. Turnham is an institution in Alabama politics, and our great state should feel privileged to have such leadership representing the city of Auburn and especially Auburn University." Pete received a standing ovation from a full house in Beard-Eaves Memorial Coliseum and he said, "I have always had a deep love for Auburn. We have the greatest University in the World, and I will continue to do everything in my power to see that nothing ever changes that fact." Pete said it was "the greatest honor I've ever received." Many friends and relatives were there for the luncheon to honor him and for the hooding at the service, a very proud moment for Pete, and his family.

PETE AND AUBURN PRESIDENT WILLIAM V. MUSE

In 1976, The Easter Seals' Alabama Special Camp for Children and Adults (ASCCA) was opened as a year-round camp on 236 acres on Lake Martin in Jackson Gap. It serves children and adults with mental and/or physical disabilities and the mission is to help people with disabilities achieve

PETE WITH 23 FAMILY MEMBERS PROUDLY PRESENT AS HE BECAME "DR. PETE."

equality, dignity, and maximum independence. Pete sponsored an Act, which became law in July 1995, making an appropriation of $343,804 from the Alabama Special Educational Trust Fund to be used for the support and maintenance of the camp.

In September, Pete received the Meritorious Public Service Award on behalf of the citizens of Alabama from the Montgomery Advertiser. The award was presented to Pete for his "integrity representing only the highest ethical standards; effectiveness in promoting and protecting the interests of those he represents; vision for a better Alabama that extends beyond the day-to-day passing of bills; trustworthiness in dealings with fellow legislators and the public; commitment to serving the public, not just political expediency; and diligence in consistently meeting responsibilities."

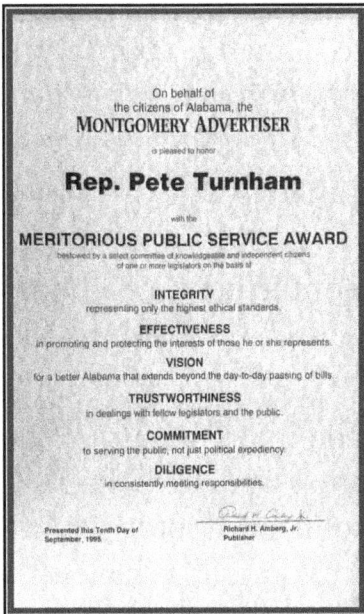

On November 2, 1995, the American Association of Adult and Continuing Education presented Pete the 'Presidential Award for Exceptional and Innovative Leadership to Adult and Continuing Education' for his outstanding achievement and contribution to the field of adult and lifelong education. The award is the group's highest honor. His work and influence increased the state appropriation for the adult education line item from $375,000 to over $4.9 million. He led the way in the creation and eventual legislative passage of Alabama's Workplace Education Tax Credit, which served as a model for the entire nation. Employers who sponsored or provided an approved adult education program qualified to receive a 20% credit on their state tax bills, an incentive for the work force, as it reaped significant and long lasting benefits, and for the companies, realizing an increase in productivity, quality, and worker satisfaction. In his role as "Dean of the Alabama Legislature," he sponsored and strongly supported the Alabama Education Act of 1990. With the passage of that act, Pete solidified Alabama's Adult Education Program with the creation of a state Adult Education Advisory Council which he at one time chaired. The council included state department heads, civic leaders, and key members of business and industry. He was also responsible for the creation of the Alabama Adult Literacy Resource Center and a standardized adult education curriculum.

In November, just before the Auburn-Alabama football game, Pete and Albert Metzger reminisced about a meeting a half-century earlier in April 1945. Both were second lieutenants in the Army when Pete led his platoon to rescue Metzger and his men who were pinned down by Nazi machine-gun and rifle fire. Pete had volunteered for the dangerous mission because he and Al had become good friends after going through officer training school together at Fort Benning. Laughingly, Pete said, "Even though he was an Alabama man and I was a graduate of Auburn, I still helped him. I crawled up to him on the front lines where he was pinned down. We were all scared to death." Al had said, "If you get us out of here alive, I'll fence your farm." According to Al, Pete wanted to get a big farm, but barbed wire was expensive. Pete said, though his troops got Al and his men out safely, he never got the chance to take Al up on the deal, saying, "I had wanted a farm, but I couldn't afford it. I never did get one."

In May 1996, Pete was present when ground was broken for the new Lee County Health Department being constructed near the Justice Center, to be opened the following spring.

Some of the many bills Pete had sponsored and seen made into law during the 1996 session were: To provide for the suspension or revocation of drivers' licenses for the failure to pay child support; To establish, in Lee County, a Motor Vehicle License System in the office of the Judge of Probate to process motor vehicle title and license applications, transfers, and renewals, and to collect and remit license fees, taxes, and monies due the State of Alabama and to the county; and to alter, rearrange, and extend the boundary lines and corporate limits of the municipality of Auburn in Lee County.

Turnham Green

In 1997, Pete and Kay made a trip to England with the Auburn veterinary school to observe veterinary schools there. While in London they visited Turnham Green, the ancestral home of the Turnham family. The surname Turnham was first found in Middlesex where the family was first referenced in the year 1194, when Robert de Turnham held Turnham Green in Chiswick. The name means 'Old English turn,' 'circular', probably denoting a U-shaped bend in a river, + hamm 'water meadow' or ham 'homestead.' Turnham Green was a village on the main road between London and the West, recorded as 'Turneham' in 1235 and 'Turnhamgrene' in 1369. In November 1642, the Battle of Turnham Green was fought nearby during the first English Civil War, resulting in the Parliamentarians blocking the king's advance on London. King Charles I's Royalist force of up to 13,000 men met a 24,000-strong Parliamentary army at Turnham Green, one of the largest gatherings of opposing forces ever assembled on English soil. Very little fighting took place, the battle more a standoff between the two opposing forces, broken only periodically by a series of small skirmishes. Despite the sizable armies assembled, neither side lost more than about 20 men each; but, strategically, it was a crucial turning point in the war, as Parliamentary forces gained a tactical advantage over their anointed king. The Parliamentary army's blockage of London forced the king to retreat to Oxford, which would become his official base for the remainder

of the war, and, indeed, would prove decisive in successfully curtailing the Royalist advance on London for the duration of the war. Both sides appreciated the strategic, economic, and psychological importance of securing the capital. Hence, the failure to seize London was arguably pivotal in Charles I's ultimate downfall.

Today, Turnham Green is a public park situated on Chiswick High Road in West London. Christ Church, a neo-gothic building designed by George Gilbert Scott and built in 1849, stands on the eastern half of the green, and a war memorial, unveiled on November 13, 1921, and telling of the Battle of Turnham Green, stands on the eastern corner. On the south side of the park stands the old Chiswick Town Hall. In the famous novel by Charles Dickens, *A Tale of Two Cities*, a passage mentions

"...that magnificent potentate, the Lord Mayor of London, was made to stand and deliver on Turnham Green, by one highwayman who despoiled the illustrious creature in sight of all his retinue." Turnham Green tube station, which Pete and Kay rode to reach Turnham Green, is situated on Chiswick Common about .6 mile to the east of the park on a street named Turnham Green Terrace, and is the terminus of route 440.

Wrapping Up A
40 Year Career

꧁

Some of the Acts passed into law which Pete sponsored in 1997 were: To provide for a cost-of-living increase for certain persons and those receiving survivor benefits from the Employees' Retirement System who were employed by Auburn University; To make a conditional appropriation from the General Fund in the State Treasury to the Department of Agriculture and Industries in the amount of $5,000,000; To make an appropriation from the Education Trust Fund in the State Treasury to the Alabama Sports Festival; Relating to Lee County, to provide for the establishment of a consolidated and unified system for assessing and collecting taxes under the supervision of an elected county official designated as county revenue commissioner; To provide for a wireless enhanced emergency 911 system (mentioned previously, the 70 cent charge for connecting 911 to wireless/cell phones); To authorize Lee County and the City of Opelika to perform certain actions for the purpose of economic and industrial development; and, To make an appropriation from the Education Trust Fund to the East Alabama Child Development Center in Anniston for the support and maintenance of a program of child care, educational, health, and nutritional services for pre-school children in 14 east central Alabama counties.

At the end of the 1997 legislative session, Pete said it was the worst in his career. "The whole state should be ashamed. There was too much greed and selfishness and too many self- centered people working for their own private selfish gains without looking at the broad picture," he said. Auburn received less than a 1 percent increase in its budget, which included about $1 million in earmarked funds not requested by

153

university officials. Pete began proceedings to draft legislation calling for a constitutional amendment forcing the Legislature to approve both the General Fund and education budgets no later than the first day after the 15th legislative day. Typically, the budgets weren't voted on until the final day of the session. "When you have a $3.6 billion education budget with one and a half hours to look at it on the last day of the session, you're in sad shape. It was a disastrous session," said Pete. The education budget included percentage increases for some of the state's private colleges that were higher than the increases given to Auburn and the University of Alabama. "How do you justify that?" said Pete. "How did Tuskegee University get a 4.15 percent increase when the largest university in the state just 19 miles away (Auburn) got .91 percent?" Good friend and Lee County Senator Ted Little said, "It shows the legislators forgot statesmanship." He said members were appointed who "saw the opportunity to make splashes rather than honor the devastated ship of higher education."

Pete made the decision that year to retire from the legislature by not running for an 11th term, as did two other long serving House members, Jimmy Clark and Tom Drake. In response to questions about the future of the House Pete said, "It's going to be different, no doubt. You're going to have a newer crew. We're going to have a lot of Republicans, a lot of Democrats, a lot of ladies, and a lot of blacks. It will be a matter of who can forge the coalition." As the current chairman of the Adult Literacy Council, Pete planned to stay active politically as an advocate for adult literacy programs, saying, "There are 761,000 people out there in the state who haven't finished high school." Pete said it was tougher to be a legislator in 1998

STATE REPRESENTATIVE
YVONNE KENNEDY, D-MOBILE,
AND PETE

than when he started in 1958. "People now seem to look out more for personal needs in their area rather than looking at the broad picture. When people get a project it damages what you can do for your entire area. It used to be we looked at the overall picture. What we did for education helped all systems." He also said the House of Representatives had become much more independent from the governor in his

TALLAPOOSA
COUNTY REPRESENTATIVE
BETTY CAROL GRAHAM
AND PETE

four decades of service. In earlier years the governor dictated not only committee chairpersons, but all committee assignments. "He wrote the budget and sent it up and somebody made a motion and somebody would second it and it would pass."

His colleagues said Pete did not stride the halls with arrogance but with competence. He was as popular with security people as he was with high-salaried lobbyists because he treated them honestly and used humor to override differences. Through nine speakers of the House and nine governors, legislative analysts estimated he cast over 100,000 recorded votes and about the same number of voice votes. In actual legislative days, he spent roughly three and a half years of his life. And, not even Pete would dare project how many constituent phone calls he fielded, how many committee meetings he endured, how many pieces of legislation he midwifed, and how many budget cuts affecting education he stopped cold.

On August 3, 1998, The Alabama Department of Rehabilitation Services held a reception, attended by over 200 people, to honor Pete for "his four decades of dedication and services to Alabama's children and adults with disabilities." During the

presentations, including a crystal award to recognize his advocacy efforts, Pete said, "When I first proposed the idea of funding an Early Intervention System, some of the legislators were skeptical. They asked, 'What if we sink $3 million into this program and then it doesn't work?' I convinced them to take a chance. There aren't better witnesses than you to show that the program does work."

That fall, Pete was honored by the Auburn Legislative Action Network with its first Legislative Tiger Award presented by Auburn University President William Muse. President Muse said, "Pete Turnham sets the standard for devotion to and support of Auburn University." While in the legislature he had introduced more legislation for agriculture than any other lawmaker in Alabama's history. A strong and effective advocate for agriculture, education, mental health, and industrial development, he was instrumental in the passage of legislation developing community mental health centers, providing funding for health and educational construction, encouraging higher education and K-12 to agree to a financing formula for educational funds, and was a staunch advocate for providing a kindergarten education in Alabama.

As a member of Gamma Sigma Delta Honor Society of agriculture, a long supporter of Agriculture education at Auburn, and a supporter of agriculture in the state of Alabama, Pete received the "Friend of Extension" annual award from the county agents of Alabama in 1999. And, in 1999, as was mentioned previously, he received the "National President's Award" from the American Association for Adult Continuing Education.

When Pete first went to the House of Representatives most representatives worked out of the trunks of their cars, although Pete said he remembered his first desk and his first few days at the old House (in the state Capital building). They had nowhere to meet privately with constituents unless they were one of the four or five House leaders who had their own office areas. Greg Pappas, the Clerk of the House at that time and there since 1975, said, "He is a dear friend, known for his great sense of humor and his loyalty. He has missed being here rarely, if at all." Beth Thacker, a committee clerk since 1967, said, "I don't think you can find anyone around here who would say anything bad about Pete. He has a great sense of humor. Everybody loves Pete. He is very effective because he tells it like it is, he doesn't lie and doesn't shade the truth. That's why people listen to Pete. The people of House District 79, and indeed the entire state, owe Pete Turnham a degree of gratitude. He has given a hell of a lot to the state of Alabama." Preparing to retire, Pete said, "They say this is a part-time job, but people expect full-time legislators. Most people would be surprised if they spent a day here and saw all the work we do trying to help our constituents." One of his memories was of being the only House member to serve four full terms with Governor Wallace. He noted that the State House currently had computers, scoreboards to tally votes, and even a separate office for each of the 105 members, noting the old wooden 30-by-60 inch desks were gone. Pete left the House, with 40 years of service, as the longest serving House member in the 179-year history of the state of Alabama. One of many tributes to Pete in his last few days as a legislator was the rare naming of a bill for a living person, a $550 million bond issue passed by both Houses and christened the "Pete Turnham Excellence in Education Bond Issue."

Pete served under nine governors and he said every one was completely different. "People ask me all the time who was my favorite of the nine governors, but I say, in their own ways all were." In his words, "George Wallace ran the House for twenty years. You tried to get on key committees so you could push your stuff out, and George Wallace would pick up the phone and say, 'Put a million dollars in so and so.' I was up there one day and we went out to lunch and I got back and he was holding for me. He said, 'Put two million dollars on the bill for Wallace Community College.' He was a tough trader. We didn't always agree but I would try to work it out with him. I put a bond issue in for a hundred and ten million dollars and it got on the calendar. He called me up and said, 'I'm going to fight your bill.' I said, 'Why?' He said, 'Because I want some money for my two-year schools.' And we worked out a compromise on the phone. But all of it was alright. We just had to dig up extra money to pay for it." Pete says those two-year schools are still a big item in Alabama and he believes they are getting out of hand. After a few years many become four-year schools and he no longer feels they serve children as they were meant to do.

Pete's thoughts on some of the governors he served were: George Wallace – "Persuasive. He ran the legislature and usually got what he wanted. He was ahead of his time. He was a segregationist but made a 180-degree turn." Lurlene Wallace – "One of the best governors the state has ever had. People thought that George would be running things, and maybe he did too. But, Lurleen became strong in her own right and she did great things for the parks system, for the mentally handicapped, and for adult literacy." Fob James – "Could have been a truly great governor but couldn't get people to support his ideas." Albert Brewer – "Brilliant. He liked to work way ahead of everything. He was always working toward what would be happening 10 or 15 years down the road in the state."

When Pete retired from the Legislature his colleagues in the House and Senate unanimously passed a resolution naming Pete Turnham "Dean of the Alabama Legislature."

Moving Forward

Continuing to work full time in his business, enjoying his growing family, tending to his house, yard, garden, and his place on Lake Martin, Pete did not slow down after his retirement from the legislature. He was still in demand as a speaker; and, as a member of Phi Delta Kappa honor society of Education, the current Chairman of the Adult Education Advisory Committee for Alabama, and Chairman of The Adult Literacy Council, he championed education at every opportunity.

In May 1999 Pete received the 7th annual Boy Scouts of America "Distinguished Citizen Award" from the Saugahatchee District. The program stated, "The Distinguished Citizen Award, presented by the Chattahoochee Council, Boy Scouts of America, brings singular recognition to an individual who has rendered outstanding service to the community, state and nation."

1999 brought more sadness to the family when Pete lost his brother, Carl, in May, and his brother, Bill, in December.

When Pete celebrated his 80th birthday on January 1, 2001, he received the following letter from his son-in-law.

Words for Pete on the Occasion of his 80th Birthday

Dear Pete:

*Many others will focus on your countless attributes that make you the special, gifted, talented and revered person that you are. **I will choose just two of your qualities in this short letter - your **patriotism** and your **generosity**.*

Someone once said that **freedom has a special taste to those who have fought and almost died that the protected will never know.** *You certainly know that special taste of freedom from your service in World War II as you liberated a hopeless people and learned to appreciate the great gift of freedom that we enjoy. Tom Brokaw called you and your warrior teammates the greatest generation this country has ever produced and I concur with him. You consistently demonstrated your love of country through your service in the reserve forces, yeoman's work as a record-setting State Legislator, and services to community too numerous to focus on any single achievement. Auburn University owes you a huge debt of gratitude for all that you have done for her. You helped turn a sleepy little ag school into one of the premier institutions in the nation. I believe at the core of all these achievements was your deep love of country and your desire for America (and Alabama) to be the very best they could be. You, Mr. Pete, are a great American* **patriot!**

You are among the most **generous** *people I have ever known. Think of the many football tickets, baskets of fresh produce, hams or turkeys, and poinsettias at Christmas that you have given away to family, friends, widows of former pastors and countless others. Your generosity with larger gifts has been substantial also as each of us has seen your huge love for us displayed through those gifts. I know our Lord smiles broadly when you reach down to help those folks who are the most needy and who, without you, might not have anyone to look after them. You, Mr. Pete, are a truly generous giver in a world of takers! Thank you for always modeling a marvelous giving spirit!*

Happy 80th Birthday, Mr. Pete, and best wishes for many more. Remember, you are still under warranty and have many more good years left!

I am extremely proud and thankful to be your son-in-law!

Love,
Bill McCrary

The Auburn University Agriculture Alumni Association was founded in 1981 by alumni and friends of AU's College of Agriculture, Agribusiness Education, the Agricultural Experiment Station, and the Cooperative Extension System. Having introduced more legislation for agriculture than any other lawmaker in Alabama's history, in 2003 Pete was inducted as a member of its Alabama Agriculture Hall of Honor.

In August, Pete and Kay celebrated with their family another milestone wedding anniversary, their 60th.

60TH ANNIVERSARY

In 2006 Pete was asked to give the devotion at the Golden Eagles banquet honoring the Auburn class of 1956, and celebrating his 62nd year as a graduate.

More sadness came to Pete when he lost his sister, Grace Moon, in May 2006 and his last sibling, Jo Hodges, at the age of 90, in June 2007.

Kay, Pete, and Carolyn

Kay began having occasional dizzy spells, a result of diabetes it was later learned, and in 2006 she and Pete felt it would be a good idea to hire someone to be with her while Pete was at work every day. Carolyn Payne accepted the position and became a wonderful companion and helpmate to Kay. Kay did not enjoy television, but Carolyn said she "enjoyed looking at catalogs, occasionally ordering from them, and talking with folks on the telephone, and there was always somebody coming here to see her." As a result, Carolyn said she spent a lot of her time watching TV because Kay stayed busy. She "drove Mrs. Kay to her beauty parlor appointment twice a week, every Tuesday and Friday, and on Tuesday, we went to Chappy's Deli. Mrs. Kay didn't do any more grocery shopping. Mr. Pete did it then Scott began to help. I took on the cooking. At first it was just breakfast and lunch, but when Mr. Pete got where he couldn't do dinner anymore, I would cook it so they would have something to eat in the evening. Mr. Pete would serve it, but then Scott began to come in, serve it, and help clean up the kitchen."

"For the first seven years I didn't have much contact with Mr. Pete. I would meet him at 8:00 in the morning and meet him at 4:00 when he would come home from work." Pete's back began to give out on him and Carolyn said, "Mrs. Kay said he had never been sick a day in his life and that's what makes it so hard on him now. He didn't know how to be sick."

"One of the first things I noticed about Mr. Pete was when he talks to you he calls you by name. He makes a point of saying your name. He would give you the shirt off of his back. They say there were times when people were invited to dinner and

Mrs. Kay didn't even know about it. They would just show up. He would just meet anybody on the street and tell them to come on in and get something to eat. Mrs. Kay said you couldn't run around in your housecoat on Sunday morning because she knew there would be people on the porch, early, waiting to see him because he would be kind to them. On weekends he was home from Montgomery and they knew he would be here, so they would just come on over. One time, after a Saturday Auburn football game, someone's car broke down out there. Mr. Pete went out and helped them change the tire, then told them to come on in and eat. They were walking around and Mrs. Kay said, 'Pete, who are those people?' He said, 'I don't know.' But, he was so glad he could help them."

The Golden Years

2009 - AUBURN DISTINGUISHED
VETERAN OF THE YEAR - PETE
AND AUBURN MAYOR BILL HAM

*I*nvitations and accolades did not stop. As was mentioned earlier, Pete was presented the 2009 Distinguished Veteran Award by the City of Auburn, presented by Auburn Mayor Bill Ham.

In 2011 Pete celebrated his 90th birthday at a party hosted by his oldest son, Tim, and his wife, Tina, in their home. He was also presented a proclamation for the milestone by Mayor Ham.

2011 - AUBURN MAYOR BILL HAM
PRESENTING PROCLAMATION
TO PETE ON HIS
MILESTONE 90TH BIRTHDAY

In 2012 on a Father's Day page in the Opelika-Auburn News, son Joe wrote the following tribute to Pete.

He came from humble beginnings off a farm, hitched a ride to college, joined the Civilian Conservation Corps and gained several Auburn degrees. He went to serve in World War II, and as a decorated solder and reservist, came home and started a successful business and family. He became a church and civic leader and for 50 years a public servant. His life and work is the epitome of Tom Brokaw's description of the "greatest generation."

My dad, Pete Turnham, instilled in me the passion to serve and help others. He embodies humility and accomplishment. His acts of intervention, kindness and advocacy on behalf of those who could never repay him are too numerous to count. While he drafted laws, consulted with governors and chaired national boards, he always took time to throw the baseball with me, go on family trips, and even now, coaches me out of bad life situations.

Not only a great dad, but, a loving husband for over 65 years – his example of family, community and faith are a beacon to me and to my own children.

Dad is 91 years old now. He still has a vegetable garden and is still teaching me the lessons of life. Happy Father's Day, Dad!

The following year the article below appeared marking Kay and Pete's 70th wedding anniversary.

Pete and Kay Turnham Mark Life and Marriage Milestone

They met when they were students at API (Auburn University) at the Baptist Student Union in 1941. Pete came off the farm in Chambers County, Alabama and Kay from the big city of Birmingham. World War II was underway and Pete would enlist in the ROTC and prepare for his role as a future Army officer. Kay would continue her education. They married on August 30, 1943 and not long after, Pete shipped off to war in Europe.

Their new marriage survived the war and Pete returned home to his wife Kay. They made a home in Auburn and raised 4 children here. Pete and Kay attained their Bachelor and Master's Degrees from Auburn and became part of the fabric of the area serving in many facets of leadership.

Kay became a lab technician then a teacher and Pete an Extension Service Dairy Specialist and later a businessman. Pete and Kay have a lifelong devotion to the church, starting out at Auburn First Baptist and later as charter members of a small mission church, which is now Lakeview Baptist Church. Today they are members of Parkway Baptist.

Kay opened her own Nursery School which she ran for nearly 20 years and went on to teach in public schools where she retired as a teacher at Beauregard School. Pete went on to public service, serving a record 40 consecutive years in the Alabama House of Representatives.

The milestone of their 70th Wedding Anniversary is still one of their great life achievements. Pete and Kay have lived in the same house on Moores Mill Road for over 60 years and still have a vegetable garden.

Kay and Pete were honored at their church, Parkway Baptist, the weekend prior to their anniversary and spent their anniversary weekend celebrating with their family.

On February 17, 2014, the movie "The Monuments Men," directed by George Clooney and starring Clooney, Matt Damon, Bill Murray and John Goodman, premiered and Pete was once again in the news. As was mentioned earlier, the movie told the story of some of the greatest art works of the world, estimated to be worth $8 million at the time and mostly from France, hidden in the Neuschwanstein Castle. The castle, built by King Ludwig II near Germany's border with Austria, was where Pete and his platoon were sent soon after VE Day to guard the stolen art until the art experts, depicted by the stars in the movie, catalogued and crated the pieces, then, sent them back to where they belonged. Soon after the movie came out the Auburn alumni news magazine ran a feature story on the part Pete played in the event. A friend from Monroeville, remembering an article George Thomas Jones had written about his part in the story, showed Jones the article about Pete. Jones, like Pete, was a 1st Lieutenant in the war and was commander of a platoon of 30 men stationed in Garmish, about 40 miles from the Neuschwanstein Castle. When the art was discovered Jones and his platoon were sent immediately to set up two armed roadblocks, one across from the dirt road leading to the castle and the other at the front courtyard leading to the entrance. After Jones was shown the volume of art in the castle he realized it would take a long time to do the necessary work. But, with no explanation, after two weeks he and his platoon were ferried back to Garmish. For 70 years he had wondered what took place following that event, and, after reading the article about Pete he had the answer. Because of the volume of art pieces found, it would take a great deal more time to catalog, pack, and transport them than was originally thought. That required a larger guard unit, and Pete's unit was 200 men strong. Jones' grandson, Matt Moorer, has a high school friend who works in the same office complex as Pete's son Joe, and Matt and Joe arranged a meeting for the two men. Matt drove his grandfather to meet and visit with Pete at his office in March, a warm and long overdue meeting of two men from rural Alabama in their 90s who had waited for 70 years to learn of their unusual connection and to share their stories.

On March 19, 2014 Pete was presented with a Resolution by the Senate of Alabama for his "Outstanding Lifetime Achievement." The resolution cites his service in WWII, his successful business, his devotion to his family, his 40 years of service as a member of the Alabama House of Representatives, his continued work in his occupation, and the immense respect earned for his tireless dedication and exceptional abilities. The final paragraph reads, "Be it resolved by the Legislature of Alabama, both Houses thereof concurring, that Mr. Pete Turnham is highly honored and commended, and this resolution is presented to him in deepest admiration and appreciation, along with sincere best wishes for continued success in all future endeavors." Senate Joint Resolution No. 85, adopted by the Legislature of Alabama on March 19, 2014. Act No. 2014-272

After almost 73 years of marriage, Pete lost his beloved wife, Kay, on April 21, 2016. They had raised four children together and had six grandchildren and five great-grandchildren. Their marriage was truly one of love and working together, Pete supportive of Kay's teaching career and Kay supportive of Pete's business and political life. Pete says he still feels Kay's presence and he misses her every day.

On May 13, 2016, Pete was honored as the recipient of the annual Wiliford S. Bailey Award by the Auburn University Retiree Association. Named in honor of Dr. Wiliford Bailey, the founder of the association and former Auburn University president and professor, "the award is used to recognize someone who has made contributions to public education, made contributions to the welfare of education retirees, and is an all around good citizen and member of the community, another Wiliford Bailey," said Dr. Gerald Johnson, AURA board member, at the presentation.

Memories and Thoughts From Pete's Children

Diane – Do you remember going to the Union Building (at *Auburn University*) on Sunday for lunch? (*In the 1950s and 60s*)

Tim and Joe – Oh, Yeah.

Diane – We ate Maryland fried chicken. It was so good. You had to wait in line for a long time, but it was cool inside.

Tim – They had those big goldfish in the pond (*Ross Square, in front of the Union Building*). That was the only place in Auburn to eat.

DIANE, RUTHMARY, TIM, AND JOE

Diane – Yeah. Everything else in Auburn was closed. We didn't have air conditioning until I was 14. There was a big window unit air conditioner in the kitchen, but when Mama was cooking it wouldn't do a bit of good. But we sure did enjoy the food.

Tim – We had a gas furnace here in the hall. Dad built a rack to go over it. He would put blankets over it at night, let them get real hot, and come wrap our feet up in them.

Diane – "Hurry and get in the bed. I'm coming, I'm coming!" He was lots of fun. I remember that!

Tim – Daddy took me hunting and fishing. And, all those things, when I was growing up, were so special. As a small child, I remember I knew approximately what time he would get home, and I would wait at the window looking for him. I would run out and jump up in his arms.

Diane – He always supported us. To come from as humble beginnings as he did, he still would come to my ballet recitals. There was no question about it. I remember one time I forgot my little pipe cleaner sparkly tiara, it was on my bed, he came home and got it, and ran it back up to me. He supported both the boys in baseball and basketball. He was a good baseball player, and Mama played basketball in college. We had a flat area right outside where his bedroom windows are now. He put up a creosote pole and basket, and we would go out there and shoot.

Ruthmary – Basketball was a way of life around the Turnham household. You, Tim and Joe, are good players, and so was Daddy. As a matter of fact, when we were all at home we sponsored the 'Turnham Invitational', and played some fun basketball games!

Diane – Do you remember when we would be getting ready for bed? It would be getting late, and we would be getting on our pajamas on a Thursday night. Daddy would be getting home at 9:30 and we'd say, "It's almost 30! It's almost 30! Get in bed quick!" We didn't want Daddy to find us up at 9:30, which was really late on a school night.

Tim – It was important that we eat together as a family each night, we enjoyed it, and the blessing was always said. One of the frustrating things for Mother was when the phone rang. The phone was right beside where Daddy sat at the dinner table.

Joe – It was a rotary dial phone on the wall behind his chair.

Tim - She would encourage him to not answer it. But, if that phone rang, he was going to answer it. Sure enough, it would be somebody needing something, and I have never seen a person get so excited to be able to help someone else. He would light up like a Christmas tree! Also, I've never heard Dad say anything derogatory about anyone. He finds what is positive about them and that's what he talks about.

Diane – I used to love watching him talking to Mama at the table. It was a happy time. He talked about all that had happened during the day.

Joe – I remember Albert Brewer and George Wallace coming by the house.

Diane – Mama said he told her about 8:30 or 9:00 one night, "By the way, Albert Brewer is coming to have breakfast with me in the morning. We're going to have so and so." Then he said (*after seeing the expression on her face*), "I'll fix it! I'll fix it!"

Tim – There was a gentleman who lived across the street from here, on the corner, named Colonel Louis J. Compton. Every morning he would come over and sit at the table and have a cup of coffee with us.

Diane – And he would get Ruthmary to drink milk.

Tim - When there was inclement weather, he would drive us to school. He was the father-in-law of General Hal Moore. Hal died a couple years ago and was living in that house. Mel Gibson played him in the movie ("Monuments Men").

Diane - His son and daughter and I were of similar age. One time one of them asked Tim how long he was here for. Tim said, "What are you talking about?" He said, "Well, how long are you going to be here?" Tim said, "I'm going to be here forever. This is my home." Because they were in the military they moved, and it was all they understood. Mama used to love to tell that story.

Joe – Julie Moore was Hal Moore's wife. When they were at base command somewhere, she found out it was just a couple officers who would go and inform a lady her husband had died. She started the tradition that officer's wives would accompany the informers and comfort the women. She got Hal to assign those volunteer wives to go with the informers.

Diane – Daddy's Army Reserve unit was in Opelika.

Tim – I can remember when I was growing up I would go over there with him, and they would put me in a little military uniform, when I was five or six years old.

Diane – He would go to summer camp, and sometimes we would go with him. It would be like our summer vacation. We would go to Ft. Bragg, North Carolina, and rent a little apartment or house.

Joe – Do you remember when we went somewhere out West and got to see Irene Ryan, 'Granny', on the "Beverly Hillbillies"?

Diane – When we went to Ft. Bragg it was one of the happiest times in my entire life. Daddy was away on business during the day, and he would come home about 4:30 or 5:00 o'clock. Then, we would go to a park and have a picnic. Mama and Daddy would watch us while we played, and, to me, it was just heaven. Do you remember we would have potted meat salad sandwiches? And one time we went to Ft.

Leavenworth (*Kansas*). At Ft. Leavenworth I remember going to the old part of town where there were a lot of warehouses. I thought it was like a cowboy town where they would 'shoot 'em up'.

Joe – The board chairman for Macon County Development Authority is Mark Innis, and his late mother, Ann Innis, had worked at Fort Benning, Georgia. She and Dad had become good friends. She was one of the general's secretaries at Fort Benning when Dad was in the Army Reserves. I mentioned her to Dad one time and he said, "I loved Ann. She was so good to me. I was struggling with my four little children, working, traveling, selling, and doing my reserve duty. One weekend I was having the hardest time getting over there, and I called Miss Ann. She called my commanding officer in the reserve unit and said, 'The general has asked for a special assignment for Major Turnham this weekend'. When I finally got over there, Ann said, 'Pete, I need for you to help me with some filing'."

Tim – When I was young Dad and I used to hunt back up toward I-85, which didn't exist then. All that was just open land. And, we belonged to two private fishing lakes here in town, Lake Ogletree and Lake Auburn. We fished, and fished, and fished. And we ate what we caught.

Joe – Daddy told me that at one time white tail deer in Alabama were virtually wiped out. This was early in his career, I guess in the 60s, and whoever was the long time head of the conservation department went to him and asked if he would help sponsor legislation for the reintroduction of the white tail deer. I think about all the hunters today. Dad was one of the ones who helped pass the legislation that reintroduced the white tail deer to Alabama.

Tim – They would not let people hunt for years.

Joe – Because they were an endangered species. We were going out Moore's Mill Road to get on 431 by Lee County Lake one day. Dad said, "You know the story about that, don't you, Joe?" I said no. It's a huge lake. He said some people came to him one time and said we need a place for the public in Lee County to fish. He had worked well with the Department of Conservation, but they said they just did not have money in the fund for one county to build a lake. But, they told him there were some counties that were allocated money for a public lake, and they never used it. They said he would have to call all those counties and get them to turn their money back in, or give written notices they would not use the money to build a lake. Nobody thought he could do it. But he was such a snake charmer that he went and got enough counties to agree to give the money back, went to the Department of Conservation, told them, and they got enough money to build the Lee County Lake.

Diane – He probably knew people in each county where he had worked and who he could call.

Tim - I was fifteen when I left home and went to military school. Back then everybody was smoking. Dad was driving through one time, came in my room, and I was smoking a cigarette. He didn't say anything to me, but for months after that I got a letter almost every day from Mother with an article about smoking in it. I got the message.

Diane – Another thing I remember is that every Christmas Eve we would go back to Daddy's house in Abanda. They hauled all of us up there and back. We would draw names and exchange gifts for a while, then there got to be too many of us to do that. And we would go there on Easter afternoon and have a big egg hunt. We would have it behind and up a little ways from the cemetery. It was up in the woods and I was only four, and I was scared to go up in there. And Tim was a baby.

Joe – One day recently Carolyn and I were in Dad's room and he started telling about when he was an extension specialist. He said someone would call and say, "Pete, we sure do miss you. When are you going to come to Selma and check on my 'whatever'?" He said he always stayed with someone in the area. Some had indoor plumbing and some didn't. "I'd take my slop jar with me", he said. He kept it in the car in case he needed it and said some had plumbing but it didn't always work. I don't know if he could take a bath.

Diane – We could walk to school and we had carpools to get to our activities.

Tim – I had a bicycle.

Joe – Auburn is a small town.

Diane – I can remember taking all my ballet stuff, riding my bicycle to the campus when Mother was a graduate assistant, and being so tired I could barely stand in my toe shoes.

Tim – I could come home twice a semester from Marion Institute, and I would hitchhike. I wore my uniform and that helped. Mama and Daddy would say, "How did you get home?", and I'd say, "I caught a ride."

Diane – Another thing I liked is that they taught us a lot just 'in the going'. You know how the Bible says, "As you go, tell your children the scriptures."

We had to do chores and I'm so glad. If I baked cookies, I had to clean it up. It was my job to clean the kitchen because Mama might have a baby on her hip, be helping another with homework, and be stirring okra. She couldn't do it all.

Joe – A neighbor and friend of mine, Jay Lamar, is the Executive Director of the Alabama Bicentennial Commission. Alabama was founded in 1819. I was talking with her one day and remarked that Dad had lived literally for almost half the life of Alabama and, for probably seventy-five years of that, he has been actively involved as a part of Alabama. One of the historical times he was part of was when John Patterson was Governor and they were cleaning up syndicated crime in Phenix City.

Diane – Oh, I remember that. I would hear Mama and Daddy on the phone and they were just real emotional about it. I don't remember what they said, but I knew it was bad, and I knew they were working on it. I was a little bit scared. I could hear it in their tone of voice.

Tim – John Patterson's dad was the attorney general over there and they (*the mob*) murdered him in an alley. That's when they sent in the National Guard and just wiped them out. He ran in 1958, was elected governor, and beat none other than George Wallace.

Joe – You know, Mom had a Bachelor's degree in early childhood education and a Master's in education.

Diane – Her first degree was in science, Laboratory Technology.

Joe – She had her own school, she wanted to go back to teach in public school, but she didn't have the block courses. She was a teacher's aide and was more educated than all the teachers. So, in her late 50s, she went back to Auburn and got all her block courses, then got her Master's degree. I was about 20 then. I remember coming home one afternoon and Mom was having a study hall, and I bet she had eight or ten college girls in there. Here I was, and my mother had all these good-looking education majors looking up at me and I was in awe that my mother had brought all these girls to our house. She said, "Y'all meet my son, Joe", and I thought, "My mother is pretty cool!"

Diane – I remember seeing a letter I think Mama wrote to Tim, and she said she had been real blue about something, but she said, "Thankfully, your Daddy is cheerful most of the time." And it's true. Now, he could blow up. He had a temper if he was pushed and pushed and pushed. What he did was, he didn't let it out little bit at a time. He'd wait. Mama said Daddy was a born leader. He could calm a group of disgruntled people, in the legislature, church, anywhere, and get them to a consensus.

Joe – I was campaigning in Sylacauga or Childersburg. For some reason I was in a car dealership, when one of the managers came out and said, "Joe, I'm so and so and I'm a Republican, but I'm going to support you. I was in your mother, Miss Kay's, nursery school, and your mom helped me." I run into that all over the place. That sort of thing is a great testimony to my parents.

Diane – The man who cleans the carpets here was in Mother's nursery school, and he just cried when Mama died.

Joe – Going back to the war… I think Dad's battalion was supposed to be re-assigned to the Pacific when the European war was over. And, he also thought his guard unit was going to be called up to go to Korea.

Diane – I remember feeling terror. I was standing on the front porch and Mother was talking to someone about the Korean conflict. I was probably three years old and I can remember feeling terror because Daddy was my emotional rock. I remember pulling on Mama's dress saying, "Mama, Mama, is my Daddy going to have to go to war?" I think I would have died if he had had to go.

Joe – And when he was in the reserves he was an intelligence officer. I think they put him on active duty for a while and they were doing intelligence work during the Bay of Pigs with Kennedy in the early 60s.

Diane – Mama had us watching TV and said, "We may go to war and we need to pray about this." I can remember the seriousness of it.

Joe – I remember Mama telling about living in the dorm during the war (*WWII*). A lot of the girls got married before their husbands went to war and she said she could remember nights when she could hear screaming and wails when a girl had gotten a formal notice that her boyfriend or husband had been killed.

Tim – Somebody would get the call during the night.

Diane – They would post a list on the bulletin board in the hall and the girls would find the names on it.

Joe – One day I was reading about the movie "Monuments Men". In the promotion for the movie was a picture of the Neuschwanstein Castle in Germany. Dad has a picture of it and he had said there was some art in it and his company guarded it. When I saw the movie promotion I printed it and took it to Dad. He said "Oh, yeah. That's the castle we guarded. I had a company and we took over from a single platoon which had been guarding it for about a week before we arrived." I put it together and called a friend of mine, Phil Rawls, a senior AP writer for Alabama. He loved Dad and when his son was working on his Eagle Scout project he interviewed Dad for part of it. Dad was still going to the office with Tim every day, so I called him and told him Phil was going to send a writer to interview him, and a photographer. The article went national. When the article came out he got a call from a man in Monroeville, Alabama. The man was George Thomas Jones, the leader of the platoon which guarded the castle which Dad's company relieved! They had never met each other, and that man's grandson drove him to Auburn to meet Dad. They talked for hours, and there was an article written about their meeting.

When I was chairing the Democratic Party for the first time in the late 90s, I would go to a courthouse somewhere to visit with the local officials. Many, many times, especially in rural Alabama, I would meet an elderly clerk or tax assessor and he or she would say, "Joe, your dad used to call on me. I loved him. He would get all my courthouse forms for me." I saw a prominent area veterinarian the other day who owns several vet clinics now, and he said, "Joe, I didn't get into vet school when I first tried. We called Mr. Pete, your dad, and he got me in."

Dad got to be close with the dean of the medical school at UAB. There was a girl from rural Alabama who had great grades, was valedictorian in her high school class, I think she finished at Auburn, and she wanted to get into medical school. Dad talked with the dean and he said, "Pete, she's on the bottom of the list, but because of you, I'm going to let her in." Years later the dean told Dad, "She's one of the top medical research scientists and one of the best medical students that ever came through here, Pete. I wasn't even going to let her in here, and you told me to take a chance on her." I have heard stories like that literally dozens of times.

I met a businessman one day who did all sorts of tax investments. He agreed to meet with me because he said, "I got into some trouble and could not get into Auburn University, but your dad went to bat for me and I got in." Today, he is making millions of dollars.

Tim – I have a similar story. This guy could not get into medical school. His dad was a doctor, called Dad, and Dad got him into UAB. He operated on me about three years ago for an emergency appendectomy. My appendix had almost ruptured. Thank goodness we knew him and could call him, and he met us at the hospital and did surgery.

Joe – I remember Daddy telling me one time the House was in session in the old historic chambers (when you look out the windows you can see the steps that go down to Dexter Avenue) when Martin Luther King Jr. gave the speech on the Selma to Montgomery March in the 60s. There was real heavy security, obviously, and they wouldn't let anybody leave because of the crowds. He remembered opening the window and seeing Dr. King and everyone right there from that vantage point, from the state house looking to the back. The black members of the House and Senate respected Dad greatly, and he respected them. Even though Dad didn't represent Macon County, he used to help Tuskegee University (Tuskegee Institute at the time) with their state appropriations, because, at one time, they would not let the black college presidents even appear before the Ways and Means Committee. He went through pre civil rights, the civil rights movement, and post civil rights. When he went to the legislature it was all white, all male, and all Democrat. When he left, it was Republican, Democrat, black, white, men, and women, a very diverse legislature, and he survived a 40-year transition of Alabama history. We have most of the House portraits dating back to 1958 or 59. When you look at them you see a lot of change. You see congressional giants, such as Richard Shelby, Bill Nichols, Tom Bevill, all served with Dad, along with former Governor and House Speaker Albert Brewer who was then a young House member.

Tim – Daddy sponsored the bill that established community mental health centers. He wanted to de-stigmatize mental health issues and to bring mental health help directly to communities. And, he also sponsored the public kindergarten bill.

Joe – He handled all the legislation for years and years for adult and vocational education, especially for adult literacy. He really believed in it. I think it was the Abanda experience and seeing people growing up to be adults who couldn't read, write, or sign a contract. He knew, even in the 80s and 90s, how prevalent illiteracy was in Alabama.

Diane – Mama would meet adults and foreign people at the library and teach them to read.

Joe – He was given their (*adult education*) Lifetime Achievement Award, a scholarship at Southern Union, and somewhere else. The scholarships were established in his name by the Professional Adult Vocational Association.

Ruthmary – Lots of people asked me if Daddy being a Representative caused any problems, and I can only say emphatically, NO! I wouldn't have had it any other way. I enjoyed traveling with him on campaigns and various occasions.

Diane – Because of that kind of thing it has afforded us privilege of certain kinds; to be accepted without question, to be respected, with maybe a few privileges to get into things. I can't think of a certain incident, but I think that is part of the way it has affected us. But then, the other side of it is we couldn't go out to Morrison's to eat as a family because people would hound him so.

Joe – It sets the bar for your behavior. My son's name is Pete Matthew Turnham and he goes by Pete Turnham. He has said, "Dad, everybody knows Pop," or "Everybody tries to compare me to Pop." He loves it but…

Diane – When they enrolled Pete Matthew into Wright's Mill Road School someone said, "Pete Turnham? You know Pete Turnham is not enrolling in the first grade!"

Joe – One day we were in the den, Dad sitting in his chair, and Mom was in there as well. Pete Matthew came in and Dad said, "Sport, how is it going with the swimming and diving?" (*Pete Matthew was on the swimming and diving teams at AU from 2014 to 2018.*) Pete Matthew said, "Good. We had our fall training camp." Then Dad said, "What all did you have to do?" Pete Matthew said, "Everybody had to learn the Auburn Creed, and if any team member could not recite it, they would have to swim punishment laps or something else. And, a couple of them didn't remember it." Dad said, "Well, I had old Dr. Petrie for a class!" (*Dr. George Petrie {1866-1947} was from Montgomery, obtained a Bachelor of Arts degree from the University of Virginia in 1886, followed by a Master's degree in 1987, and most of his studies focused on languages and moral philosophy. He completed his PhD at Johns Hopkins University in 1891, and accepted a position at Auburn, then the Agricultural and Mechanical College of Alabama. A historian, professor, and coach of Auburn's first football team, after 43 years as a professor and administrator, Dr. Petrie retired in 1942 and wrote the Auburn Creed in 1943.*) Near the end of Dr. Petrie's career he was asked to teach a current events course about Europe. He was an authority on the history of that part of the world and about how the Third Reich was coming into power. Much of the reason it was taught was so the students who were volunteering to serve in the armed services would understand the history behind why they were going into WWII.

Diane – And Mama was in the class, too.

Tim – One of Dad's college roommates, Jimmy Thompson, started a company,

CCC Associates in Montgomery. He got Dad to buy stock in his company when he started, and Jimmy was very successful. It grew tremendously and Jimmy went to China and built factories which employed thousands of people. He built hospitals and school systems, and all the employees could send their families for health-care and education for free. Dad was the largest non-involved shareholder and served on the board of directors for years, and Jimmy took him and a few others to China one time many years ago. One of the divisions of the company was CAFFCO in Montgomery.

Joe – In the 90s and early 2000s I was still doing politics, and I would be in Montgomery and go to the state house a lot. No matter who the lobbyist was, they would say, "Joe, how is Mr. Pete? I just want you to know, your father was the most professional and nicest person. (Several said) He hardly ever supported what I did, but every time I asked, he would let me go into his office and he would sit down with me. He was never ugly about it, and, if he said, 'I can't be with you,' or 'I can be with you,' he kept his word." Even still, the older ones now will say, "Joe, they don't make them anymore like Mr. Pete."

There were some non-state agencies that would get a state appropriation because of a special need, like Tuskegee. For years, because of his service in the military, Dad would get an appropriation for Lyman Ward Military Academy.

Tim – And, for Marion Military Institute.

Joe – There were some new members who were challenging the appropriation one year, trying to strip it out. But some astute members ran out of the chamber and got Dad, because they were preparing to vote on an amendment and they had almost enough of them to agree on stripping the line item. Dad rushed back to the well of the House and gave this patriotic speech saying, "These young boys will be fighting. I was in the war, and we counted on the military!" Everybody cheered! The amendment failed and the appropriation survived another year. Every year everyone came to the chamber for Pete's Lyman Ward – Marion Military speech! I got a call one day from Bill Baxley, the former attorney general and lieutenant governor, and he said, "Joe, we won a class action case for 'something', and part of the judge's order is that a hundred thousand (or whatever) go to two schools in East Alabama. I want to give this money in honor of your dad. What can I do?" I talked to Dad and he wanted Lee Scott Academy, where I had gone to school, to have half, and he wanted Lyman

Ward Academy to have the other half, and that's where it went.

Diane – Who called Daddy Peter Rabbit, because he was always in such a hurry?

Tim – I believe it was Bowen Braswell, over in Phenix City.

Joe – Daddy and two other legislators were invited to the White House. I think it was something to do with the Panama Canal. They met with President Carter in the oval office, and toward the end of the meeting Dad said, "Mr. President, I'm from Auburn." The president said, "Pete, Auburn's my mother's second home." Lillian Carter was the fraternity mother at the Kappa Alpha house for years. And, they had a great talk about Auburn.

Pete

Though because of his health Pete is confined to his home now, Carolyn says he still has a lot of company, and when people visit she says, "he knows all about them," a testament to the man who has been interested in, loved, and cared for people for 98 years.

When asked what Pete is really like people have often said he's exactly what he appears to be. Kay said he was a loving and hard working husband. Joe said he is a good father who has always made time for his children. A fellow legislator, Dutch Higgenbotham, said he was an honest friend who always did what he promised. And former Auburn University President James Martin said he was a true public servant who was warm, friendly, and caring.

Some of the many words of praise said about Pete through the years are...

> He is a class act, a gentleman in every way.
>
> Mr. Pete is a legend.
>
> He saw and made a lot of history.
>
> Far above average in intelligence.
>
> A tremendous help to me.
>
> The permanent legislator.
>
> A man of high integrity.
>
> He doesn't lie or shade the truth.
>
> He really enjoys doing things for people.
>
> A best friend.

Pete is the kind of person who is magnetic.

He took me under his wing.

Thoroughly honest and dependable.

He was my mentor.

Pete's accomplishments in the legislature were huge.

Always uplifting and never complains.

He has a great sense of humor.

Known for his loyalty.

He always made time for me.

He is loved by so many.

His life is a gift that keeps on giving.

Everybody loves Pete.

And, from the Bible, James 3:18 describes Pete well….

"Those who are peacemakers will plant seeds of peace and reap a harvest of goodness." (CEV)

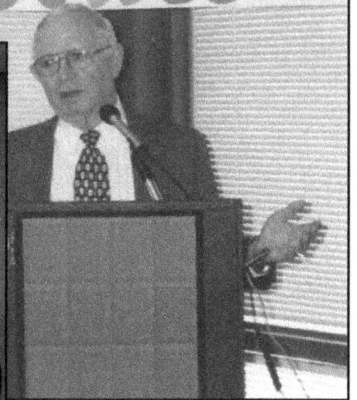

Epilogue

*P*ete and my mother, Marguerite Turnham Romine, met as teenagers at a family reunion. Though they were distantly related, sharing great-great grandparents, they bonded and formed a close lasting friendship. When my mother married my father, Jim Romine (James Harold, known as Harold while at Auburn), the bond became closer because Dad was a 1940 Agriculture Education graduate of API (Alabama Polytechnic Institute, later Auburn University). After graduation he went to work in Birmingham as the Farm Radio Leader for the Alabama Extension Service, writing and airing two daily farm and home programs aired through WAPI in Birmingham and WCOV in Montgomery, furnishing coverage of 4-H Club, FFA, and farm events throughout Alabama. Pete, an active student in the clubs and events of the agriculture department at API, sometimes worked with Dad on news events.

When Pete and Kay married they were still students and had no car, not uncommon in those days. My parents attended the wedding and loaned their car to the newlyweds for their honeymoon.

Mr. Pete

When Pete returned from WWII his ship docked in New York and he took a train from there to Atlanta, where my parents then lived. Kay drove from Auburn to my parent's home and there the two reunited after being separated by war for a year and a half.

L-R - JIM, KAY, AND MARGUERITE

L-R - PETE, KAY, AND MARGUERITE
WITH BABY ANN

The closeness of the two couples continued to grow as children arrived and the love of family and tradition grew stronger. As mentioned in the book, a particularly looked forward to event was the Auburn - Georgia Tech game played in Atlanta every other year when Pete and Kay would travel to Atlanta and the two couples would attend the game together.

Pete affectionately called my mother 'Cuz', and that endearing term transferred to me as well. When I arrived as a student at Auburn in 1962 I knew my 'home away from home' was with Pete and Kay. If Pete was on the campus and saw me, or if he saw me heading to a football game in my band uniform, I would hear him holler, "Hey, Cuz!"

We celebrated the big life events with each other, birthdays, marriages, and graduations.

L-R - ANN, KAY, PETE, AND
MARGUERITE AT A FAMILY
WEDDING - 1995

I am often in Auburn and when there I would stop by to see Pete and Kay. In March 2016, I stopped to visit Pete, and in our conversation I asked if anyone had written his story. When he said no, I said it needed to be done and he said, "Thank you." A short time later I showed up with a recorder and our work began. Having grown up knowing Pete as just my special "Cuz" who loved his garden, worked

184

LEFT TO RIGHT: TIM, COUSINS FROM MT. SHASTA, CA.
(DAUGHTERS) IRENE, ANNIE, AND (MOTHER) LILLIE TURNHAM,
PETE, MARGUERITE, KAY, DIANE, (MARGUERITE'S DAUGHTERS)
SUSAN, ANN, AND JOE AT PETE'S AND KAY'S
50TH WEDDING ANNIVERSARY - 1993

L-R - ANN, MARGUERITE,
PETE, AND KAY
AT MARGUERITE'S
80TH BIRTHDAY - 2000

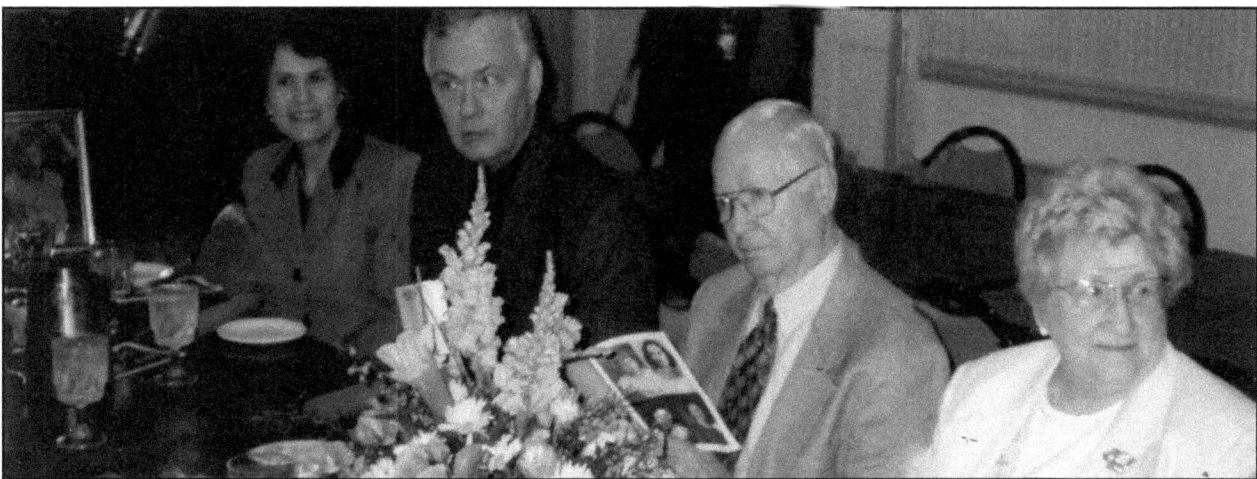

ANN AND CECIL WILDER, PETE AND KAY - 2000

hard, and was in politics, learning about the whole person was an education for me. I had no idea of the impact he had on so many and of the true capacity of his love for all. After two and a half years of research and many visits with Pete, the book was finished and so was his life. When listening to the recording in his last few weeks, Pete only had me change two sentences, leading me to feel that together we had done a good job.

ANN, PETE AND KAY - 2009

185

Bibliography

The Early Years

Online – Wikipedia – Abanda CDP, Alabama – U.S. Census Bureau, American Factfinder, Retrieved 2014

The Alabama Future Farmer, Published by Alabama Association of the Future Farmers of America, December 1937

Leaving Home

Draughn, Ralph, Jr.; Hughes, Delos; Pearson, Ann; Lost Auburn – A Village Remembered in Period Photographs (Montgomery: NewSouth Books, 2012)

Online – Wikipedia

The Opelika-Auburn News, Gene Stevenson, "Depression Era Work of Auburn CCC Remembered with Pride," March 6, 1995, Page A5

The War Years

The Seventy-First Came to Gunskirchen Lager; Wyman, Major General Willard G., 1945

The Birmingham News; Sparrow, Hugh W., "Two Work Together Again – Turnham, Horton Served in War, Now in House," April 11, 1965

Getting Established and Making a Home

The Auburn Bulletin; Colburn, Amy L., Bulletin Founders Day Supplement, 1981

The Sunday Eagle; Campbell, Cathy, November 15, 1987

Mr. Pete

Entering the Alabama House of Representatives

Online – Encyclopedia of Alabama, Resource on Alabama History

The Southern Star (Ozark, Alabama); "Lee Legislator Says Education Alabama's Top Problem," April 16, 1959

The Montgomery Advertiser; "Legislator Dons Brass at Benning," November 28, 1959

Newspaper Article – Name Unknown; Stallworth, Clarke, July 12, 1960

The Columbus Enquirer (Columbus, Georgia); Levy, Bill, "Russell Mental Health Group Adopts Plan to Operate Clinic at Opelika," April 30, 1963

Montgomery Advertiser-Journal; Ingram, Bob, "Floor Leaders Prove Effective – Administration Pushes Rated Taxes by Press," September 8, 1963

Birmingham Post-Herald; Chamblee, Leonard, "Auburn's Pete Turnham to Head Rehab Group," October 26, 1963

Newspaper Article – Name Unknown; Badger, Eddie, "Schools – Industry Link is Described," March, 1964

Southern States Energy Board

Online – Wikipedia

Southern States Energy Board – A Golden Anniversary History of Service to the Southern Region; Brown, Dr. Canter, Jr., Nemeth, Kenneth J., 2010

Saturdays and Auburn Football

Online – Wikipedia

Continuing to Move Forward and Take on More Responsibility

Opelika Daily News; "Needed Change," Editorial Page 2, March 29, 1965

The Tuscaloosa News; Davis, Paul, "He's Waiting Governor for Help," Page 1, July 22, 1965

Lee County Bulletin; "Turnham Taking Army Course at Ft. Benning," October, 1965

<u>Lee County Bulletin</u>; "$125,000 Approved for Lee Public Lake," Page 1, November 21, 1965

Newspaper Article – Name Unknown; "EDI Thoughts"

Continuing to Serve
<u>Roanoke Leader</u>; "Kiwanis News with Dr. Van", 1969

<u>Opelika Daily News</u>; Blackman, Wink, "Turnham Predicts New Plant for Area"

<u>Montgomery Advertiser</u>; Dakin, Milo, " 'Wet' Option Bill Passes in House", Page 1, August 6, 1969

<u>Farm Bureau Publication</u>; October 1969

Election Time Again
<u>Montgomery Advertiser</u>; Dakin, Milo, May 9, 1971

Newspaper article, Name unknown

<u>The Opelika-Auburn News</u>; Page 1, May 4, 1971

<u>Auburn – Opelika Daily News</u>; August 9, 1971

<u>Auburn – Opelika Daily News</u>; August 27, 1971

<u>The Mobile Register</u>; December 10, 1971

<u>The Opelika-Auburn News</u>; Blackman, Wink, Page 1, February 6, 1972

<u>The Birmingham News</u>; October 6, 1972

<u>AARP News Bulletin</u>; Page 1, January 1973

<u>The Auburn Bulletin</u>; Davis, Owen, Page 1A, April 26, 1973

Continuing to Expand Duties and Responsibilities
<u>The Opelika-Auburn News</u>; Grimes, Millard, 1974

<u>The Auburn Bulletin</u>; Page 1B, May 26, 1974

<u>The Opelika-Auburn News</u>; Grimes, Millard, January 24, 1975

<u>The Birmingham News</u>; April 27, 1975

Newspaper article, Name unknown, May 30, 1975

The Birmingham News; Holmes, Ralph, June 24, 1975

The Auburn Bulletin; July 6, 1975

Newspaper article, Name unknown

Honored As He Works

The Opelika-Auburn News; May 14, 1978

The Auburn Bulletin; Page 13, January 28, 1976

The Roanoke Leader; Page A2, June 6, 1979

The Opelika-Auburn News; September 2, 1979

Newspaper article, Name unknown, September 6, 1980

The Opelika-Auburn News; Page C20, January 15, 1981

The Opelika-Auburn News; Page 8, May 1, 1981

Newspaper article, Name unknown

The Opelika-Auburn News; June 30, 1982

ALAPCAE Journal; Vol. 1 No. 1, February 1983

The Opelika-Auburn News; Pool, Penny L., Page 1, 1984

The Opelika-Auburn News; February 15, 1985

The Southerner; Page 1, June 2, 1986

The Opelika-Auburn News; February 1987

Newspaper article, Name unknown

The Valley Times News; Mendelson, Mitch, March 6, 1989

Newspaper article, Name unknown

Birmingham Post-Herald; Bruer, Frank, Page C1, April 1, 1991

The Birmingham News; February 22, 1991

The Montgomery Advertiser; McCartney, Tracey, Page A3, May 15, 1991

Newspaper article, Name unknown, May 9, 1991

The Lee County Eagle; Thomaston, Carmel, Page A1, November 6, 1991

The Opelika-Auburn News; December 15, 1991

Always Pushing Forward

The Opelika-Auburn News; Harper, Samuel T., Page 1, May 20, 1992

Newspaper article, Name unknown; White, David, February 28. 1993

The Montgomery Advertiser; Ingram, Bob, May 5, 1993

Newspaper article, Name unknown; Merlini, Jim, September 21, 1993

Auburn University Outreach Update; Page 3, Fall 1994

The Opelika-Auburn News; White, William, December 20, 1994

ALAPCAE; Alabama Association for Public Continuing Adult Education News and Notes

The Mobile Register; Werneth, George, November 18, 1995

Lee County Eagle; May 1, 1996

Turnham Green

Online – Wikipedia

Wrapping up a 40 year Career

The Montgomery Advertiser; Vort, Stan, Page B7, May 23, 1997

Newspaper article, Name unknown; Poovey, Bill, 1998

The Montgomery Advertiser; Chandler, Kim, August 17, 1998

The Opelika-Auburn News; Markley, Greg, Page C1, April 19, 1998

The Birmingham News; 1998

The Golden Years

The Opelika-Auburn News; June 17, 2012

The Randolph Leader; August 8, 2013

The Opelika-Auburn News; August 8, 2013

Mr. Pete

The Opelika-Auburn News; February 17, 2014

The Monroe Journal; Jones, George Thomas, Page A7, March 5, 1915

Pete

The Lee County Eagle; November 6, 1991